Philosophical Harvest

BY

MARTIN KNOX

Philosophical Harvest

BY

MARTIN KNOX

First Published – 2025
This edition published 2025 by Novel Ideas
Brisbane, Qld
Australia

Copyright © Martin Knox 2025

The National Library of Australia Cataloguing-in-Publication

Creator: Knox, Martin, author.

Title: PHILOSOPHICAL HARVEST

ISBN: 978-1-7636472-8-2

Subjects:　　Autobiography fiction
　　　　　　Memoirs

All rights reserved

This book is semi-autobiographical and except in the case of historical fact, any resemblance to actual persons, living or dead, is purely coincidental.

This book is sold subject to the condition that it shall not, by way of trade or otherwise, be lent, resold, hired out, or otherwise circulated without the publisher's prior consent. No part of this book may be reproduced in any form, by photocopying or by any electronic or mechanical means, including information storage or retrieval systems, without prior permission in writing from both the copyright owner and the publisher of this book.

The author asserts his moral rights.

Typeset in Times New Roman 12pt by Donna Munro Graphic Design.
Cover artwork by Donna Munro Graphic Design.
Printed and bound in Australia by Ingram Spark.
Copyright © Martin Knox 2025
Publisher: Novel Ideas, West End, Brisbane.
htttps://www.martinknox.com
martinknx46@gmail.com

Martin Knox Books

Available from Amazon in Australia, USA, UK and Canada

The Grass is Always Browner (2011)
Love Straddle (2014)
Presumed Dead (2018)
$hort of Love (2019)
Time is Gold (2020)
Animal Farm 2 (2021)
Turkeys not Bees (2022)
Brisbane River Anti-Memoir (2023)
The Camel, The Lion and The Child (2024)
Energy Lessons (2024)
Nanny State (2024)
New Climate War is Real (2025)
Facets of Femininity (2025)
Philosophical Harvest (2025)
A few passages have been extracted from previous books and included in this book without referencing

Contents

CH	Chapters	Philosophy	Page
	PART 1: DISCERNING RELATIONSHIPS		1
1	End of youth	Descartes	2
2	Oldies	Descartes	4
3	My perception	Sokolov	8
4	Dancing	Religion	10
5	Family relations	Kierkegaard	13
6	Existential flooding	Heidegger	16
7	Brisbane River	Heidegger	19
8	Flood Mitigation	Heidegger	22
9	Apartment Gift	Sartre	23
10	Putting Down Roots	Sartre	27
11	Merging	De Beauvoir	29
	PART 2: FATEFUL MEETINGS		33
12	Mimetic desire	Girard	34
13	Ladders	Political economy	40
14	Love pair	Girard	42
15	Desiring Vicki	Girard	44
16	Social class	Jane Austen	48
17	The Game	Psychology	51
18	Sailing with Maria	Derrida	54
19	Oil slick	Derrida	59
20	Class differences	Class morality	64
21	Commodity Markets	Economy	66
22	Commodity speculation	Matching criteria	70
23	Grain Spread	Profiting	73
24	Vulnerable	Marx	78
25	Girls Spread	Exchange	80
26	Love Match	Balancing assets	82
27	Consent	Economic strategy	84
28	Commodifying love	Monetizing choices	87
29	Delivery contract	Agreement	89
	PART 3: ACCEPTED		93
30	Fling	Oversight	94
31	Retaliation	Revenge	107
32	Livestock judging	Saussure	100

33	Weather	Heidegger	102
34	Janetta	Heidegger	105
35	Flying	Heidegger	107
36	Volkswagen	Heidegger	109
37	Rita	Levi-Strauss	111
38	Neighbours	Levi Strauss	112
39	Chess with Sarah	Levi-Strauss	115
	PART 4: ADAPTED		117
40	Stranger in a Strange Land	Levi-Strauss	118
41	Rabbiting	Nietzsche	121
42	Conger eels.	McLuhan	124
43	Fishing	Levi-Strauss	126
44	Alcoholic beverages	McLuhan	128
45	Hanging on	McLuhan	130
46	Over Servicing	McLuhan	132
47	Survival camp	McLuhan	134
48	Artificial selection	McLuhan	137
49	Astronomy night	McLuhan	140
50	Nuclear power	Camus, Foucault	142
51	Quantock Ponies	Foucault, Popper	146
52	Water divining	Popper	148
53	Energy supply	Kuhn	151
	PART 5: ADVENTURES		153
54	Stopping without brakes	Physics	154
55	Acorn boutique	Kuhn	156
56	Driving to Panama	Derrida	158
57	Serengeti balloon safari	Debord	160
58	Mekong River journey	Baudrillard	162
59	Pole vaulting	Heidegger, Baudrillard	163
60	Government overreach	Baudrillard, Debord	164
61	Flow	Mihaly	167
62	Time dilation	Einstein	171
63	Governing climates	Baudrillard, Debord, Girard	175
64	Closing the Short	Girard	178

Dedication

I dedicate this book to
my family: Zoe, Tessa, Amani, Uly and Dorian

Acknowledgements

I am indebted to the following.

Donna Munro has looked after the formatting, cover design and publishing.
Dave Jones provided valuable feedback on political matters.
In the 'Matters Arising' group at Brisbane's University of the Third Age, issues were discussed.
Sunnybank Hills Writing Group read and discussed Cold War events.

Author Bio

Martin Knox grew up on a farm in Somerset, England. He rode a horse and played rugby. He graduated as a chemical engineer from Birmingham University. His work with energy was in a nuclear power station, in petroleum engineering in Canada, in coal mine development and energy transportation. He researched alternative systems of government at Imperial College, London. He became a high school teacher and wrote science textbooks with energy emphasis, published by the Queensland Department of Education.

This book is his thirteenth book published. He has been writing fiction and satirical novels full-time since 2013: speculative, love, politics, government, crime, sport, totalitarianism, science, energy and technology. He is involved in public policy-making; has proposed an underground railway for Brisbane; developed ideas for mitigating flooding of the Brisbane River; and an anti-memoir of his spiritual enlightenment following Friedrich Nietzsche. He has written about the philosophy of climate science from the phenomenological viewpoint of Martin Heidegger. He frames the net zero campaign as a superpower climate war. He discusses current issues at U3A and has read philosophy texts at the University of Queensland. He attends community development forums.

He blogs ideas from his books and relates them to events in the news. He writes letters, plays the guitar, plays chess and walks in the park by the river where he lives.

He reads classical novels, watches movies and enjoys *The Big Bang Theory*.

He is divorced with children and grandchildren.

PART 1:
DISCERNING RELATIONSHIPS

My aim is to show that boy-meets girl has powerful motivations not usually transparent but with important consequences. Memoirs are presented sometimes in an order that events could have occurred, embellished with a little fiction.

To predict and oppose river flooding, I imagined engaging an interlocutor, Grania. Together we applied phenomenology and identified a list of problems for action by the river authority. They were problems overlooked by conventional Cartesian analysis, leading into adoption of post modernism, existentialism and Heidegger's phenomenology.

CHAPTER 1 END OF YOUTH

I was about 14 when I realised I was attractive to some girls. They began to notice me and asked me what music and pop stars I liked. At school I wore the uniform but when I went to a party I wore stovepipe trousers and winkle-picker shoes, with an Adam Faith haircut.

Attracting girls was important and I began to act up to their interest with tough behaviours on the rugby pitch, with my friends and at dances. I showed off to girls when I could, wanting to reveal my strong physique and natural intelligence.

The girls did the same, showing off their figures, hair and social intelligences.

I blamed my genes for my aggressiveness. I even threatened my Dad when he tried to use me like a tool. I avoided confronting my mother because she always won. I put on my red shoes when I was to be best man at my brother's wedding and they insisted I wear black shoes. Eventually I gave in after they attacked my lack of loyalty and social restlessness.

I was kept busy with school, farm chores, socials and accompanied my father around the farm and on trips into the local town, to attend the selling of our livestock in the market.

I seldom had time to consider what to do next or to imagine what it would be like to be older or in a relationship with a girl. When I speculated about the future, it was filled with my ambitions, such as owning a sports car and foreign travel. It never occurred to me that I would be a member of our family into old age. My parents' wisdom was to demand a social morality which was petty bigotry. My empathy did not extend to wondering about their lives, wants and dislikes.

The moral virtues drummed into me were hard work, honesty, thrift and kindness to women. It seemed like a recipe for endless tedium and demeaning drudgery. I was warned about laziness, theft, drinking and fast women.

The girls I desired were beautiful, friendly, smart and curious. I was shy and didn't have siblings or friends that I opened up to. Faced with a rigorous activity schedule and little social contact, I became mildly depressed when I was 15 and 16. I steeled myself to perform my routines because there was a light getting brighter at the far end of the tunnel, when I would leave home and go to university.

I didn't know what a university would be like, but I hoped it would have the freedom I craved for. I worked hard at my school work to gain university entrance. I suspended normal living while I studied for the exams.

I was unable to change my life, because it was decided by adults. I was concerned about the Cold War and I needed adults to do something to stop it before it would be too late. I hoped that my education would make me persuasive and enable me to earn big money, but my progress was unbearably slow. I needed to be logical, educated and have money.

CHAPTER 2 OLDIES

While I was struggling to make a start in the adult world, my grandparents tried to keep up. Grandpa had shown me his towering rage, that my mother had spoken of.

'He has a nasty temper,' she said.

'Take that, you bastard,' Granpa shouted, smashing the hen-house door into pieces with a hammer. He had been trying to fix it, but he was no longer adept with hand tools and had struck his thumb.

The problem was that his skills had declined. There were other ways of defining it but this indictment of Granpa's misbehaviour in the UK was in the tradition of the analysis by philosopher Renee Descartes (1596 - 1659). Descartes would identify the problem answering the questions: what, why, how and what if? Repairing of the hen-house had been required, but was no longer possible because Granpa had smashed it up through bad temper. It was too late now and it would be necessary to begin again with a replacement door.

My mother had regarded it as a duty to ask her parents over on Sunday and Grandpa had driven them over in his car. Grandma and Grandpa came to Sunday lunch at our farm. I was too little to help and we had given up on the hen-house. My father would mend it later.

Most of their time with us was spent with them working out our names and ages. It was a disruption to our normal activities, our hobbies and games.

'You must be on your best behaviour,' my mother would tell us. It was a strain.

They would try to engage us in conversation, but we said as little as possible knowing that they would soon give up if we remained silent. They would stay for the afternoon and if there was a birthday, or Christmas or Easter, for the giving of presents.

Their farewells were heartfelt because we weren't sure whether we would see them again.

When they had gone, my mother would be sad.

'They might not be able to come again,' she said. It never occurred to me to ask them what they did to occupy their days. They seemed to spend most of their time sitting. I wondered if it was old age that stopped them moving or whether it was old age that made immobility respectable.

My father's father was already dead. His mother was too frail to travel far from her home in Yorkshire at the other end of the country. My father would visit her once every year, taking one of us children with him, to visit his brothers, sisters and their families.

My mother's mother went into hospital with a heart condition and died.

On the day she died, Grandpa cried and sobbed all night in a bedroom where my brother Harold and I were trying to sleep.

Later, Granpa and a woman friend visited us, but it wasn't the same without Gran..

I was used to death because on our farm animals died sometimes and others died from sickness or accident. It seemed unlikely that I would ever die because I was still growing and no end was in sight.

After an accident, they took away Grandpa's driving licence and he stopped coming. We visited him at home once, but the lady who lived with him was unfriendly. I didn't see him for a while and then he had a heart attack and died.

I never was close to a grandparent, like I was with old Mr Askey, a neighbour. I played chess with him and watched his television.

The old people seemed to lack abilities, waiting around like cardboard cut-outs. It never occurred to me to do anything with them. About all I would do was ask them about the old days and then they would open up with a lot of stuff I didn't understand. When I asked them to explain, I regretted it because they would go on and on. Mr Askey said little. He puffed on his pipe with a twinkle in his eyes and moved his chess pieces. He made mistakes sometimes and allowed me to take back a bad move.

'Will you always live here?' I asked my mother.

I imagined that my parents would stay the same when they got old and I would be able to talk with them about things in the same way as I always had.

'No. When you have grown up, you will move away and get a place of your own. Your father and I will retire and get a place so Harold can take over the farm. '

I knew their plan was for me to leave the farm and get a job. Grandad had two brothers who been left at the home farm, but they had fallen out.

'Brothers always fall out in business,' my mother said.

'Will you live with one of us?' I asked my father.

'No,' he answered. 'We don't want to be a burden to any of you.'

'What do you mean, a burden?'

'It's a lot of work to look after old people. They can't do all the chores or cooking, cleaning and shopping. There are places called residential care where old people are taken care of. We will go there. You will not be a burden to us.'

Renee Descartes' philosophy would prescribe that an old person would be looked after by someone, a relative. An old person couldn't decide his or her own fate.

When Dad turned 65, he and mum moved into a cottage they had bought near the farmhouse. The landlord rented a farm to my younger brother. Harold stayed in the farmhouse with his wife. Dad was able to do a few light jobs and keep an eye on the place. Mum's housework was unrelieved. She continued to cook and clean as she always had. After about 10 years, Dad got mild dementia. It was too much for Mum to care for him. She and Harold moved Dad into a residential home for men with dementia. It seemed to me like a hell, without privacy or young people. I complained that we were leaving Dad there and I was unpopular for saying so.

My age was a barrier with my parents and we were unable to share experiences. We lived in different worlds and we had little we discussed together. I asked questions to find out what it would be like to be an adult, but I couldn't imagine being over 20. But I questioned how to lead a good life and how to be valued by others.

I spent a lot of time thinking. Usually I got stuck and problems remained problems. Philosopher Renee Descartes' analysis in the

17th Century was the first problem-oriented philosophy and it recognised the necessity to apply thought. Until then, the almighty was relied on and it was usual to follow traditional ways. Descartes' thinking was full of doubt and he didn't allow for observers to have any effect. I didn't help Granpa with the henhouse because I didn't have a better method. If I had thought of it, I would have taken the hammer away from him and knocked in the nails myself. It would reduce the task to small activities able to be performed by each of several helpers. That was the most usual method of analysing problems by the Cartesian method of mind over matter.

Descartesian problem solving was a blunt approach leaving little to the imagination. It was years before I learned a different approach that allowed everyone's perceptions to be different.

CHAPTER 3 MY PERCEPTION

I learned Descartes' method at university in engineering studies. Descartes used reason and the power of the human intellect to discover knowledge. He used the Scientific Method, dividing subject from object. I learned that problems were about objects and my view of these was my perception, as the subject. It was a duallist method and deeply flawed because it supposed there is a world out there, possibly with gods, in which I was the subject and physically removed but able to observe and analyse natural factors. Descartes' philosophy did not allow for perception other than by the subject.

Philosophers discovered that perception was a series of steps that would lead to a solution. Granpa's perception was the basis of his categorisation of the problem. There were five states of perception in a five step process, which Sokolov called: stimulation, organization, interpretation, memory, and recall.

Granpa's ability had been wrongly considered as appropriate to fix the hen-house door. Like Goldilocks, he expected his methods to be just right for the job. Categorization is a fundamental cognitive process that enables us to navigate and make sense of the complex world around us. By grouping objects, concepts, and experiences into categories, we can identify patterns, establish relationships, and communicate effectively with others. Sokolov (1920 – 2008) regarded perception as distinguishing novelty.

Whether it's temperature, taste, size, or complexity, humans have a tendency to seek out options that are neither too much nor too little, but rather fall within an ideal range. The process would find a moderate solution. There was nothing moderate about grandpa's attack on the door. Although perception of aging is a conditioned reflex, Granpa was unable to perceive his own aging.

My perception of the problem with the henhouse lacked stimulation. I perceived the door was broken but I lacked organisation to consider alternatives. Nor was I reminded of a previous similar situation and nor could I recall the best way to tackle this one.

I am holding back my story here to recognise age-appropriate judgements made by myself and others. Family members use these often to guide younger and older members for their safety and consideration of others. I was young and unable to warn grandpa of possible disastrous consequences. The last time the door broke, poultry escaped and the fox found several of the hens.

I have wanted to dismiss Descartes' approach because of his dualism. I did not expect the admission of God to be useful. I have wanted to allow in many other approaches, such as Kant's will and reason and Heidegger's phenomenology. Instead of invoking a subject-object canon, they allowed causation by remote and peripheral elements. Sokolov's perception was important because it distinguished novelty and allowed me to be creative.

My aim is to include philosophical elements that relate to my analysis of the various topics, assisting understanding of events and my continuity. The key to fixing a hen-house door was to allow various stages of perception.

CHAPTER 4 DANCING

It was 1963, I was 17 and I contemplated studying for a degree in religion at Lampeter Bible College in Wales. I had gone there in the school holiday the previous year, to try college life and find out if I would like to join the Church of England.

Our family attended church on religious holidays. I had been an altar boy, unobtrusively helping our vicar run services. I was being prepared for confirmation in classes he ran. He had nominated me to go to Bible College.

Fifty of us, males and females, spent two weeks together at this summer school at the college. The college's students were on summer vacation and we each had a room, ate meals together in the refectory and prayed together in the Church. Prayer was my least favourite activity. There were about half a dozen older persons directing us with boring lectures.

When we arrived, they fed us then we sat us on benches in the Church choir, facing the pulpit with the organ behind us. We prayed, mumbling the words from our prayer books, then listened as a preacher read the lesson, then they indoctrinated us in our learning and what we could and couldn't do.

I had heard it all before, last year.

'Are you going to join the church?' a student asked me.

'No. I'm here for the girls,' I said.

'Really?'

'Yes. Just watch me.'

We were a compliant group, remaining silent and refraining from pranks. I wanted to talk to the others, especially the girls, but I remained silent, out of respect. Our parishes would receive a report of any misbehaviours.

I went with a group to play table tennis and there I met the girls. They were attractive and fun, except one who said she was engaged to someone at home.

We found a record player and Buddy Holly records and we danced with more energy than skill.

Dancing awoke something in me. I had gone to old-time dancing evenings locally with my mother. It was sedate and all the females were middle-aged.

Sue danced with me at Lampeter and she was red hot. She danced me to a standstill. We did a dance she called a 'cake-walk' in which we swung our legs up from the hip, alternating sides together, faster and faster, in time with The Shadows, until we were exhausted. After that we jived to music by Buddy Holly and to pop songs, such as The Shake and The Twist.

Sue was an inspiration. I was shy and hadn't done these dances before but she pulled me on to the dance floor and showed me the moves. When slow music played, I held her, but she wouldn't kiss me even when we went outside.

The dancing was tremendously stimulating. I had found myself at last, after years of hanging back and letting others be the centre of attention. The dancing seemed to empower me. I felt I had become a more powerful version of myself, as if I had realised I could from studying Nietzsche's philosophy of will to power.

I spent most of my free time with her and we progressed to holding hands. She was a terrific companion, smart and full of fun. I was besotted.

I met up with her for dancing every evening.

The two week summer school passed pleasantly. Sue kept me at arms' length.

One of the clergy spoke to me.

'Are you having a good time?'

'Yes, thank you.'

'You could stay here for three years and study to become a clergyman.'

'Would I work for the Church afterwards?'

'Yes. You would get a job, first as a curate and help a clergyman in a country parish somewhere. You would assist with baptisms, confirmation, weddings and funerals. Do you think you would like to help with those?'

I couldn't think of anything I would like less, but I kept it to myself.

'Yes.'

'There would be weekly services. You would help with readings, singing and communion.'

I was familiar with a clergyman's activities from my role as altar boy.

'Would I get a parish of my own after a while?'

'Yes,' he enthused. 'You could do what you like, within reason.'

I tried to imagine becoming a turned on vicar.

I would want to be in a relationship with a girl who could become my partner and this would mean having children. I imagined Sue could be my wife. The girls had come to the summer school to meet potential partners. In those days girls could not become clerics. Sue complained about that.

'It's not fair,' she said. 'I could do it as well as you.'

On the bus going home one of the clergy spoke to me.

'I hope you will consider studying religion. It's good work and a good life.'

'Thank you. I will.'

But I never took up the offer of a place. I was 17 and wanted to set the world on fire.

When I got home, I tried to get Sue's number at the other end of the county, without success. We were a long way apart.

The life of a clergyman seemed very narrow. I wanted to experience the world of engineering and foreign lands.

I chose to go to Birmingham University, where I would learn about petroleum technology and could get well-paid work and a girl of my choice, without the church's involvement. I chose my own way. I sometimes wondered what had happened to Sue.

CHAPTER 5 FAMILY RELATIONS

Our family sometimes went on Sunday mornings to Church of England services. I was the only altar boy and officiated at communion on these occasions. We didn't go regularly because there were farm activities such as cows calving which had to take precedence. But when it had been decided we were going, there was a scramble to put on our Sunday clothes and cram into the family car, an old Austin. When we arrived outside the church we would hear the drone of voices raised in a hymn. We stealthily crept past the font into the nave. The singing would stop, as everyone would turn and watch the seven of us perched along a pew bench, doubling the congregation. Then the service would be resumed.

When we returned home, the hen-house still had to be fixed and it was too late for Sokolov's reflex perception. The method now in favour was to try Kierkegaard's (1833 – 1855) religious passion. This meant far more than reading the words of the Gospel — it meant living them; it meant action. Abraham had taught that faith is a personal experience between the individual and God and this experience transcended reason.

Granpa could have done more than remember reading the words of the Gospel — it meant living them. With his faith in mind, he could have engaged in virtuous action, such as hammering. Faith is a personal experience between the individual and God and this experience transcends reason. Many interpreters have construed Kierkegaard's philosophy as ruled by passion.

But it was too late because the broken henhouse lay in a heap on the ground.

The sermons of our vicar from the pulpit told us how we should live every week, with passion. Life was too brief not to put everything we could into what we did.

I construed passion as sex and tried to understand Lady Chatterley's lover, banned from sale but freely available from school friends.

I went to Birmingham university and afterwards worked in Canada and then Australia. I returned to visit my parents and siblings but we had grown apart. Our family had never planned together and my siblings would not discuss where my parents would go when they had to become dependant on others in old age. I was appalled by the place where they locked in my father and I said so. There was bad feeling. No matter how I looked at it, old age seemed unpleasant.

In Australia, I had two children with Rita. When they finished school they collected their T-Shirts and CDs, moved into flats and went to university. Rita and I had few common interests and after 30 years with me, she left me and married a man she had known at university. My part of the divorce settlement was to keep the apartment where I was living by the river in Brisbane.

Our daughter Tegan bore a girl, Alexa. She separated from her African man, worked for the WHO and lived in Switzerland and on Pacific Islands. Sarah had divorced, living and working in England with her two boys, Nico and Lucas.

When my father died, my mother moved into a private residential home. After that my correspondence with the rest of the family mainly concerned his legacy which was managed by trustees and by the solicitor who was executor of his estate.

My father's estate was divided equally between his children, but distribution could not take place until my mother had died. In the meantime the executor managed we five siblings' inheritances. After about 10 years, when my mother died, I distributed the final amount in the same way as for previous amounts. I distributed 25% to each of Sarah and Tegan, retaining 50% for myself and Rita. I could have retained the money to be distributed in my estate when I died. But receiving the money earlier when it could benefit them in raising of their children seemed judicious.

I trusted my daughters that they would not spend the money they inherited frivolously, or lose it to a partner. I looked for a means to gift them the money, so they could repay debts such as mortgages and acquire investment properties.

I bought a second apartment in my apartment building, to give it to the two girls.

CHAPTER 6 EXISTENTIAL FLOODING

Learning to live by the Brisbane River was dramatized by occasional catastrophic flooding. My dasein, applying Heidegger's phenomenology, included my intent, requiring strategic thinking about my family members. They did not come into the traditional Cartesian analysis of flooding that other people were using. It focussed on the details of each flooding event, without statistical analysis of the existential problem.

I had two apartments and both could be flooded. I realised the possibility of flooding as a shock. It took some time to digest the Council's Flood Risk information and decide what could happen to each apartment. I would continue to live in the one on the ground floor, in which the basement had been flooded. I considered whether to give the other apartment I owned on the first floor to my daughters.

We had to decide triggers for evacuation. We could continue living there until the electricity was turned off and then cooking and chores would become difficult in both apartments.

My abiding concern was to have a refuge where we could go if we had to evacuate from the Atrium buildings. We had been fortunate in 2022 to be able to stay with a friend, but such an opportunity might not come again

If there was a room available, we could go to a hotel in South Brisbane. With a car or a taxi we could take our computers and connect to the internet there. We would set off early, to avoid traffic jams on Montague Road and other arterials.

The risk of being flooded in Unit 1 was small and I could possibly continue living there if the basement was flooded. After all, the living area had never once been flooded in the 25 years I had owned it. In my view obstruction of the river by silt and construction was getting worse, but it was only an impression. I was sceptical about climate change and demonstrated the courage of my convictions by giving little credence to forecasts it would worsen river flooding.

When I contemplated the river flowing into my apartment, I imagined evacuating as I did in 2011 and 2022, and if the water came higher, drowning was an alternative. Drowning could be attractive, compared with living an evacuated life among strangers, without the comforts of home. I perceived life in Unit 1 as transient and fragile. I would feel no obligation to participate further than being immersed under a deep flood and drowned, by voluntary suicide. I felt an obligation to younger people to make my exit stoically, rather than tragically. Drowning was a contingency, not what I wanted. The worst outcome was that damage to the building could not be insured. Repairing the walls, floors and ceilings would be a big job, taking a long time with much expense.

My perspective of the river and its floods was affected by my age of 79. Heidegger's philosophy always included death as a possible outcome and he wanted us to be prepared for it. The prospect of death, strangely, was liberating. I contemplated my death but I didn't bring Tegan in on it yet. It seemed negative, but consideration of my Being-towards-death would make my Dasein whole. Heidegger's analysis had German words that were difficult to translate but with meaningful concepts.

His existential viewpoint provided a post modern viewpoint, that went behind the scene of usual Cartesian analysis. Speculation about death had ontical existential meaning, real and limited, taking precedence over other events. Any moment could be my last, my utmost possibility for being, to the point where my life became impossible.

My being-towards-death was an unusual posture for someone of my age. I did not announce I was preoccupied, but some people guessed. A clue was that I was not accumulating new possessions, merely repairing and renovating small damage. Things that had taken my time in past years, such as replacing worn and broken gear, didn't matter anymore.

Age would eventually disable me. The worst of it would be that caring for me could detract from the lives of Tegan and Alexa, if they stayed with me. I wanted to exit as independently as possible, fighting the flood as I went under.

I was still considering what to do with Unit 6. It depended on what Tegan and Alexa wanted. I had lived by the River for 23 years and experienced two major floods. I felt experienced enough to summarise recent events and predict the future in a memoir of my investigations and findings. I hoped to attract readers to understand how my living by the Brisbane River could be improved. My alternatives included moving up to Unit 6, because it was set higher in Atrium. The alternative I preferred was for my daughters to have Unit 6 to live in and they would not want me to move up there.

CHAPTER 7 BRISBANE RIVER

I also needed to prepare for future flooding, to know when to evacuate, if I could.

'What do you hope to get from phenomenology?' whispered Grania, my imaginary friend, who helped me undertake the phenomenal analysis.

'I want our analysis to reveal the subjective Dasein of the Brisbane River, as it would be experienced by each of us,' I said.

'Do you mean the river-ness of it?' asked Grania, adopting a suffix used by Heidegger.

'Yes. Something like that,' I said. 'Hopefully I will find more potential for the Brisbane River by phenomenology than I have found so far by Cartesian objective analysis.'

I often wanted to consult with an experienced Brisbane River dweller, who could engage with the questions I had about river flooding. Grania had experience of phenomenological analysis of droughts in the river catchment area. She was smart and pleasant.

'Descartes' observer is so doubtful he doesn't see potential for mitigating river flooding,' Grania said. 'We need Heidegger's method for that.'

'Yes. Phenomenology is like wearing sunglasses that cut out the 'glare' of unprospective low potential,' I said. 'The observer engages in 'what if' subjectivity. For example, the river's potential could be an obstructed channel cleared of obstructions to become a better floodway.'

Later I phoned another friend, Howard. He was a professor at the university. I had kept up with him since we were undergraduates, playing tennis weekly. Like me, he was an engineer, interested in colonial history and public policy.

'What do you know about phenomenology?' I asked him.

'What for?'

'I'm trying to envisage the future of me living by the Brisbane River,' I said.

'Phenomenology is a new idea,' Howard said. 'It does to science what impressionism did to classical art: it finds more potential for pleasure in the same experience. It's controversial and the old science die-hards think it's rubbish.'

'They have attempted to observe behaviour reproducibly; to be objective; to control observation; to hide observers; to isolate subjects; to hypothesise; to falsify; to do tests blinded and double-blinded,' Howard said. 'Cartesian scientific investigations of causes omitted inferences and circumstantial evidence. They were often devoid of human values, without meaning of existence, beyond physical and biological processes. True understanding of river behaviour has been inaccessible until now.'

'Phenomenology considers intentions and meanings, looking behind scenes for potential present-at-hand, or ready-to-hand, for the analyst to enumerate,' I said. 'The analyst makes explicit the purpose of the inquiry, its provenance, trajectory, mood, ambiguities, articulation, and projected future, all in an open slather of eclectic subjectivity. It replaces dry cognition with interpretations that can be used.

'It's a big task. I have a friend, Grania who has been doing phenomenology work.'

'That's ideal. Don't hold back from River events observing neutrality and refraining from trying things out,' he said. 'When flood heights are missing, make estimates. Nor will you leave buttons unpressed. You need to find out how systems work. Heidegger's phenomenology encourages us to taste a grape before buying a kilogram. When you come to a road you don't know, instead of looking for it on a map, you must explore it. Phenomenology empowers us to sample reality and conduct experiments, looking for things that could be useful. Our Being There, or Dasein, is immersed in potential.'

I thanked Howard for his advice and started work with Grania.

A few days later she came into my home office, attractive and lively.

'What intent could a river have?' Grania asked. 'It would seem to depend on whether a drought or a flood is looming.'

'In a river, water is moved to the sea by gravity,' I said. 'Every process and everything that helps the water reach the sea is useful and therefore is significant.

'Heidegger's genius was to recognise how anything useful was relevant,' she said. 'A single point of view does not have to be defined. Curiosity, ambiguity, future projection, fallenness, thrownness, moodedness and articulation of understanding are all relevant, to the extent they are useful.

'I like your analogy of phenomenology being like wearing sunglasses, cutting out the glare of low potential,' she said enthusiastically. 'It is like the epiphany I had when evolution was revealed to me in a biology class at school. Suddenly the form, size, colour and behaviour of every living thing was meant for survival by evolution. Features of animals and plants were different forever afterwards contrasting with God's purposeless handiwork. For example, a kangaroo's legs and hopping enabled it to survive by escaping pursuit through scrub. Now phenomenology reveals how the intent of the river is to flood or drought.'

'Phenomenology doesn't see the features of other philosophies,' I said. 'Evolution looks for survival features; love looks for loveliness; photography looks for appearance; portraiture looks for portrayal; phenomenology looks only for potential.'

I was pleased that we had begun to understand phenomenology. It was a different approach than the one I used to understand nature and technology. I had glimpsed improvements that could prevent the River flooding.

CHAPTER 8 FLOOD MITIGATION

When I gathered methods found by Heideggerian analysis to have potential for mitigating river flooding, there were five schemes which could benefit people living in floodable properties.

1) River dredging to remove silt and sand from river.

2) Bridge support island and abutment approvals withdrawn

3) Prevention of construction on the river flood plain that would block floodwater flow.

4) Prevention of river headwater flow by material eroded from adjacent farmland.

5) Emptying and maintaining flood mitigation pockets at all dams

Grania compiled this list, observing the obstruction of the river's flood water. She fitted flow equations to predict the effect when the river was in flood. Each of these type of obstruction would hold back flood water, preventing its escape through the river channel. The flow effects are documented in my book *Brisbane River Anti-Memoir*, Chapters 34, 33, 36, 45. I wanted the river authority to remove obstructions causing river flooding.

CHAPTER 9 APARTMENT GIFT

I had lived in my apartment in Brisbane for 16 years, with visits from Sarah, Tegan and their families. It was sometimes crowded and I considered buying another apartment in Atrium. My idea was to present an opportunity for my daughters to put down roots close to my place where I could be near them.

I waited 15 years for Dad's estate to be settled. When I received my inheritance I passed a half to my daughters and used the remainder to purchase Unit 6, a floor above. I had owned Unit 6 under a year, when the basements of both units were flooded at mid-garage level and I lost my belongings stored there. In 2011 and again in 2022 I had become aware of more possibilities for flooding than I had realised when I acquired the units. My investigation of the Brisbane River was helped by the Council's publication of its excellent Floodwise Property Report. For the first time I had become aware of risks that could be quantified for my apartments. The information was helpful for evaluating alternatives for living there with the possibility of flooding, or for moving away.

This departure into strategies for disposition of my property oriented my story to focussing on the realities of river flooding for thousands of Brisbaners living in similar circumstances. It emphasised the critical role of flood heights for damage to property and the need for all types of flood mitigation. Matters I had reviewed as having potential for mitigating flooding, such as prevention of erosion and resumption of river dredging, now assumed critical importance. There were other factors exacerbating flooding that I could investigate, such as city location, infrastructure, transport and bridges.

Tegan and her daughter came for a visit and stayed in Unit 6. She was a diligent mother, wanting to have her daughter, friends and possessions around her, with control over who could come there.

'I could live here,' she said. 'I like this apartment. Why don't you want to move up here?' she asked me.

'I don't want you to worry about flooding,' I said to her. 'I'm used to it. I'm thinking of giving the apartment to you and Sarah to share.'

'Wow, Dad,' Tegan said. 'That would be incredibly generous of you.'

It seemed natural that because I was older I should take more risk. Young termites stayed inside their mound caring for the larvae while termite adult soldiers went outside the nest, risking death. Nature protects the young.

I had no obligation to give them the apartment. I saw the situation as an opportunity for them to create roots in West End close to me. If I kept the property it would pass to them on my death, possibly in twenty years' time. Living there would enable Alexa to attend a good school nearby. Sarah couldn't return to Australia yet because she shared custody of her children with her former husband in England. But when the children left home, she might be able to come home.

'The contingency of existence (is action).'

Jean Paul Sartre

'Man is condemned to be free; because once thrown into the world, he is responsible for everything he does. It is up to you to give [life] a meaning.'

There were various ways Tegan and Sarah could share ownership of the apartment. We talked about some alternatives, such as joint ownership.

'Sharing the apartment will be good for the togetherness of our family,' I said. 'You could help each other in many ways.'

'Sharing is a great idea, Dad,' Sarah replied.

After a few weeks holiday, Sarah returned to England.

'How would you be, chancing the next flood, Dad?' Tegan asked. Unit 6 was a floor higher in the building than my home in Unit 1. 'Could you take refuge with me in Unit 6?'

'Gambling is not in my nature. It wouldn't do me much good if the water continued to rise, because evacuation from Unit 6 has to follow the same escape route as from Unit 1 and when Unit 1 is filling, the way would be submerged.'

Although her Unit 6 would be unaffected by a flood threatening my Unit 1, Tegan would be preoccupied with preparing to save her things at a time when I would be trying to evacuate into Unit 6. Friction would be inevitable.

'Perhaps you could get another place, away from the river?' she suggested.

'There is nowhere I like as much as here and moving would be expensive,' I said.

I chose to stay.

'I can always choose, but I ought to know that if I do not choose, I am still choosing.'

Jean Paul Sartre.

I needed an action plan. I would value living beside Tegan and Alexa, with potential for care as I became less able to care for myself. I was hurt that Tegan wanted me to live further away, as if my gift was without obligation even for light care or as a dry haven. There were strings to my gift and they were negotiable and not onerous.

'Perhaps you can compromise, accepting less amenity but get away from flooding.'

While I was arranging for her to live in the apartment above mine, she was proposing I move away. I lacked impetus to move my home. Living by the Brisbane River was safe enough for me. The dams were holding up; deluges had not become more frequent and it was the dry season now. With these odds, it was reasonable to continue to accept the uncertainty of the weather.

The news media sensationalised weather reporting to attract audiences. Australia is a large continent and there was usually a cyclone lurking somewhere that could pose a threat, most often offshore in the north near the equator, or moving inshore from the Pacific Ocean. The alerts broadcasted by the Bureau of Meteorology worried everyone. Cyclones were unlikely to travel into the Brisbane River catchment and waiting for a flood was interminable, like waiting for an earthquake.

Estimating the likelihood of my place being flooded was the crux of my investigation.

'The circumstances in 1893 were a fluke,' I said. 'It is very unlikely that two cyclones will again coincide over the catchment. The order of severity of recent flood years, from the most number of properties affected, was worst in 2022, 2011 and 1974. But there was most flood damage in 1974 because it was localised, with the rain falling further down the river. Our understanding of flood effects is incomplete. A flood like 1974 may not happen again for a long time.'

'Management of the dams has to contend with uncertainties.' I said. 'Dam operators are thrown into situations without previous experience. In the past, political leaders have elbowed in with their intuitions, opened the flood gates and caused mayhem.'

'Another refinement could be to dredge at the ocean outfall, decreasing water levels, which could speed up discharge of flood water.'

CHAPTER 10 PUTTING DOWN ROOTS

I was happy to live at a place I called home, where I could see my family. West End is a residential suburb within a loop of the Brisbane river. The riverside has many apartment buildings. People stroll along the river bank, or frequent restaurants along tree-lined boulevards. Traffic is kept away from pedestrians and diners at street-side tables.

It is a place I miss when I am away. I have lived in Unit 1 of Atrium buildings for nearly 25 years. Now with the purchase of Unit 6, I can have my daughter and granddaughter living beside me. It is a place where I belong.

'Roots' comes from the Latin word radix, meaning 'starting point,', I think of the root of something as the place it starts from, whether that's the root of a tree, or the root of a problem. I wanted the apartments to be a starting point for my family.

My analysis of flooding by the Brisbane River of my apartment employed Heidegger's existentialism and Sartre's freedom of the will. Sartre was strongly anti-deterministic about human choice, seeing the claim that one is committed by earlier choices as a form of self-deception to which he gives the label 'bad faith'.' Sartre was even more meticulous than Heidegger in identifying potential and denying previous choice, believing 'Existence Precedes Essence.' My own choice of living place had been made earlier by 'bad faith,' with self deception that had now revealed itself.

Starting with only a vague idea of how to use the purchase of Unit 6 to provide roots for my family, I had to imagine all the circumstances in which some or all of us would want to live there. Sartre's baleful existentialism became the framework for deciding how to resolve who would live there.

Hannah Arendt's book The Origins of Totalitarianism describes how a community like West End could be beset by private and public self-interests that deny the population rights that are enjoyed by citizens in other suburbs. For example, West End and South Brisbane were scheduled for the fastest growth in population of all Brisbane City's 194 suburbs.

I have been disappointed that the planning authorities have designated West End for fast development, with building heights exceeding planning regulations and lacking infrastructure promised. It was apparent that truth was being driven out by base lies, because lying was debasing truth.

Sir Thomas Gresham was an English financier who observed a spate of 'clipping' of slivers of gold from around the rims of gold sovereigns. He deplored the disappearance of unclipped coins and takeover by clipped coins as the driving out of circulation of unclipped sovereigns by clipped coins of the same face value but of lower value. It was deflation, with sovereigns decreasing in real value.

I had used this experience with gold currency to predict consequences in Australia of the current spate of lying in public affairs, which had taken over, like clipped versions of the truth, with lies devaluing truth. In reporting in Australia, there used to be a supply of pure truth. Then the supply of sovereign truth was corrupted by dilution with base lies. Soon all truth was withheld and only lies were available.

Truth had been driven out of circulation by base lies.

It behoves people who want transparency, truth and reason in public discourse, to detect and cancel public lying with truths, so that it will disappear. In public discussions of causes of river flooding, I would be meticulous with the truth.

CHAPTER 11 MERGING

Simone de Beauvoir (1908-1986), was a real companion in Sartre's lifelong philosophical work of existentialism, which she helped him to popularize. In her book Ethics of Ambiguity she emphasizes that to be ethical we must recognize the dual nature of the human condition not only in ourselves, but also in those we perceive as other.

De Beauvoir was a proto feminist who commented on women's challenges: *'the theme of women's vulnerability – in the first, to the process of ageing, in the second to loneliness, and, in the third, to the growing indifference of a loved one.'*

She argued in her book 'Ethics of Ambiguity' that being human means living in constant tension between opposing forces—individual and collective, freedom and responsibility, subject and object.'

The flooding of apartments 1 and 6 did not seem to interact with the other Atrium apartments. There could be a clash of interest with the shared staircase to the higher units. I made sure that people could not be trapped in Unit 6 by rising water.

Her perspective was relevant to my gift to my daughters. Part of the existential analysis of merging utility of the two apartments was to recognise each others' needs. My investigations had found that flooding of Units 1 and 6 had reasonable risks. Tegan was willing to take on the risk of Unit 6 and I would stay in Unit 1. Security would improve for both of us.

In mid 2022, Sarah and Tegan and their families were visiting me from overseas. I loved having my family around me. As we amicably made plans for the transfer of Unit 6, there was strong mutual interest.

'If Sarah would sell me her share, I would take possession and move in,' said Tegan. 'I'm not sure how soon. It depends when I can finish my job.'

Tegan would have to find another employer in Brisbane, quitting a good job in Fiji with the WHO.

'When I visit, where would I stay?' Sarah asked.

'With me,' said Tegan. 'We would fit your kids in somewhere.'

'Some or all of you could stay with me,' I offered.

'Great,' said Sarah. 'Thanks.'

She was a pretty blonde with a pony tail. She ran half-marathons.

'Every step hurts,' she had told me. 'It does me good.'

Her stoical determination had not been acquired from me, but I appreciated it.

Quiet, thoughtful, inscrutable, humorous and prickly, she worked as a senior lecturer. She liked to stand before a packed lecture theatre, presenting her views from meticulous research, cleverly reconciling opposing viewpoints on some controversial topic when feelings were running high. She was a skilful debater with formidable skills of persuasion. Charismatic, her ideals shone as she recognised the potential in others and ignored unpleasantness.

She played chess and poker well. In poker games with stakes of pennies, she took away dollars. At her university, she coordinated a large postgraduate degree programme, matching acolytes with opportunities and assessed accomplishment.

'I'm not sure how to get most benefit from your gift, Dad,' Sarah said.

'It all depends on what you want to do with it,' I told her.

'I can't return from England,' she said. 'But I can come back on holiday at intervals of about 18 months.'

Tegan could make plans to use her half of the apartment.

'I could furnish it and pay the bills,' she said. 'Sarah could pay for the time she is here.'

'Will you get a tenant?'

'If we lease it, we won't be able to stay there when we want to. Cancelling bookings and evicting tenants would be the pits.'

'If I gave Unit 6 to the two of you to share, what would you do with it?'

'I'd like to live there,' said Tegan, 'as soon as I can arrange it.' Sociable and spontaneous, she wanted it badly.

'I want to give the apartment to you two equally,' I said. 'If Sarah will not be returning in the foreseeable future, as seems likely, perhaps Tegan could buy Sarah's half share at market value, with her savings.'

Both girls had savings from an earlier partial distribution of my father's estate.

'Yes, I have the money,' said Tegan.

Sarah was reluctant at first, not wanting to convert bricks and mortar into cash, at a time when inflation was rampant.

'Tegan is taking on more risk than you,' I told her. 'Your position is good.'

I wanted Tegan to be fully informed of her prospects for the apartment. Apart from the risk of flooding, I reminded her that Brisbane City Council had approved a new bridge across the river, blocking her view of the river, from outside Atrium to the university.

There was a lot for Tegan to consider but she was a risk taker. Her planning method was to hold many prospects open and maintain flexibility until the last possible moment. Her caution was often at the expense of others, as she was not empathetic and did not realize how others felt.

Tegan and Sarah hesitated only briefly, then Tegan agreed that she would buy Sarah's share.

'Let's do it,' I said.

Tegan couldn't move in yet, but getting a tenant for the interim would be too difficult. It seemed extravagant to keep it empty, with Tegan's furniture and very few visitors.

Sarah's study leave ended and she returned to England with her children. She didn't expect to be back for several years.

We signed a three-way contract. It recorded that I was irrevocably gifting the property to Tegan and Sarah 'in consideration of natural love and affection'. Tegan agreed to pay Sarah for her half of the value and paying all the tax. It was all formalised within two months.

'It's yours now Tegan. You owe Sarah for her share,' I said.

Tegan whooped.

'Thank you very much, Dad,' he said. 'I love the apartment. I would never be able to afford to live in a place like this without your gift.'

I had given Unit 6 to Tegan and Sarah equally. Tegan had bought Sarah's share and she was making plans to move there with Alexa. I looked forward to their living above me and hoped I would see more of them.

De Beauvoir said: *'One's life has value so long as one attributes value to the life of others, by means of love, friendship, and compassion.'*

People who live on the deltas of the Ganges, Euphrates and Yellow Rivers are probably inured to regular river floods. Living in flood-prone homes on the floodplain of the Brisbane River, families have the inconvenience of floods, as the flipside of their coin toss with low cost living. Rich people could afford favourable conditions but the masses would suffer hardship and would have to either adapt or perish. In China, construction in 1984 of the Three Gorges Dam on the Yangtze River required 1,250,000 people to move away, who had lived all their lives in riverside towns and villages of great antiquity. I would continue living in the same place as I had for 22 years, with my daughter and granddaughter coming to live in the next building. In the event of a flood reaching my apartment, they could help me escape.

We never discussed what we would do if the place flooded. Tegan had been staying there in February 2022 and I had evacuated with her to John's place. Tegan would now be higher in the building, with her things better protected from flooding, than are mine in Unit 1. But she could need to evacuate, if the water cut off her exit down the staircase. I bought a rope escape ladder to hang over the back balcony gaining access through the gardens to the road neighbour's, so they would be able to climb down if the main stairway flooded.

I had given my children an apartment on the level above mine to share, hoping it would create family unity. We had talked through evacuation of Unit 1 and Unit 6, without discovering any conflicting ambiguities.

PART 2: FATEFUL MEETINGS

When I met an undergraduate girl at university, there were traditional methods of pairing off, but I experimented with new methods and devised a way of commodifying love, which I expected to develop a bond between us.

CHAPTER 12 MIMETIC DESIRE

I first met Vicki at university in the UK, at the beginning of second year, when I was 19, several years before I emigrated to Canada and later to Australia.

Trying to be social, I scanned the crowded coffee lounge for a familiar face. I had seldom come here as a fresher, because I had spent my time studying. Socialising was not my scene, but at the end of the previous year I had finished with Bridget, and needed a new girlfriend. I felt geeky and awkward.

At the far end of the room sprawled a casual group, fashionable and confident, third years from well-off families. An exceptionally good-looking girl ornamented the group. I focussed on her as I sipped my coffee. She seemed to be holding court, the centre of attention, at once absorbed and yet aloof, seeming a little bored. Her head swung her ponytail. Sincerity and good humour alternated with scepticism and ridicule. I wanted to hear the talk and tried to get closer. I pushed through the crowd towards her, apologising repeatedly.

As I neared her, I could see she was a magnet holding the group together. She sat back in a maroon silk blouse, her breasts bulging under a pattern of bunches of shiny red cherries with dark green leaves. Tight blue jeans encased her long slim legs and maroon knee-length leather boots. She was smoking a cigarette delicately, with straight fingers, blowing it upwards in a narrow jet. Other students, male and female, are smoking, too. There is a pall of smoke over the room.

From time to time, she uncrosses her legs and leans forward to tap ash into an ashtray on the table. She is talking, discussing something with her group. Her posture is self-conscious, and I can see she is making an effort to be heard amid the uproar. She seems to have a personal interest in the topic. She shows a curious mixture of strength and vulnerability. I hear her say 'Smith' and 'Wilson' in a melodic BBC voice. She seems to be talking about the threat of Rhodesia's Unilateral Declaration of Independence, ridiculing Wilson's weak stand against Smith's white racism. I guess she went to a posh private school and is studying law.

I stand to one side, where I can watch her. She looks up at me and I return her gaze, putting on my happy face. She smiles back with brilliant green eyes and looks away. She is breathtakingly beautiful and used to admiring stares. Her long thick hair is the colour of old copper, tied high at the back of her head and swings as she talks. She has slender hands, wrists and arms. On one wrist, she wears a classic gold Cartier watch, presumably an heirloom. On the other is a plain gold bracelet, a solid gold bangle, by the absence of a join mark. She is wearing jewellery worth more than most students' total possessions. Her ear is white and fragile like a seashell, with a light gold circle swinging by a chain from a stud in the lobe.

When she turns, her face is almond-shaped and fair, with a light sprinkling of freckles across the centre. Her nose is narrow, straight, and finely chiselled, with the end upturned away from a sensual mouth. A smile plays on her full lips. It is the face of an aesthete, someone with a passion for refined experiences. Her eyes are also playful, up for adventure. I get an impression of kindness, intelligence and fun.

'What do you think Smith will do when, um, Harold arrives in Rhodesia?' she asked. I was too far away to join in this conversation. She seemed accustomed to speaking in public on issues and has ideals.

'The situation will escalate, Vicki,' a student said.

A pretty name, I think. She shakes her head, ponytail jiggling. 'No. Smith will make some piddling concession, so that Wilson can save face, like promising to have an election. Wilson will claim it is, ah, a back-down.'

'Vicki's right,' I interrupted loudly, over the top of a student who is replying to her. He is surprised and falls silent. Vicki turns her head and looks me up and down. I continue, 'Harold is most interested in getting re-elected. Justice for black Rhodesians won't get many votes.' Everyone looks at me. The group falls silent as they strain to listen. 'As Vicki said, Wilson will desert the blacks, pulling out and leaving Ian Smith to crush the movement that Labour has encouraged up to now. It's a double-cross.'

Vicki nods at me thoughtfully. I kneel down and sit cross-legged on the carpet beside her. When I speak in a group, the silence afterwards always hurts and I feel rejected. It is a test of my intelligence and the buzz of conversation resumes. Vicki turns to speak to the student on her other side from where I am sitting. As I watch she asks him a question, but I can only see the side of her head.

I try to lip-read his answer and recognise some words: engineer, second year, nerd, first year girlfriend, chemistry, finished. They are talking about me and Bridget, my girl during most of last year.

Then another in the group starts rebutting my argument, stating that because Rhodesia depends on our mineral markets, economic sanctions would be successful and that is the way Wilson will go. It makes good sense and I learn from it. I have already achieved what I wanted. I have made a favourable impression on Vicki and the group. I have guessed correctly that they are not Labour stalwarts and my attack on Wilson is acceptable.

I watch Vicki's eyes and I try to imagine being her, aware of her deep beauty and unique features. Dark green irises nestle quietly but alert in her pure white sclera beneath long copper eyelashes. Her eyes retract as brow and cheeks come together in deep smiles that crinkle at her temples.

She is totally alive to her surroundings, feeling others' emotions and moods, giving her mind to understanding, rather than pronouncing judgements, her awareness composed rather than fearful. She is her own person in every way. Her friends return her smiles. I had heard that *'A woman who gets male group attention is attractive to individual males.'* I was not the only male who desired her. According to philosopher Girard, my desire for her could originate from their attraction to her. I am a victim of mimetic desire for her, caught from the others.

I studied the desire for her. It was third person desire from her other admirers and I had caught it. Their desire was covert, intensely embarrassing and they wouldn't admit to it. The power dynamics made them miserable. I was too new to the group to enter into any rivalries over her. The others wanted to reduce the conflict.

She is aware I am watching her by her lingering small smile, her feigned interest in others' conversations and the way she combs her hair through her fingers. I feel myself falling under her spell. She has infected me with desire to be with her. I wonder what subject she studies. She is too alive to her surroundings to be a lawyer. She could be an art student or maybe in education.

After half an hour, everyone gets up and goes off to lectures. Vicki passes me politely, with an encouraging smile, as if she wants to meet me, but I am too shy to say anything. She leaves an odour of wild flowers. Where her bare arm brushes against mine, my hairs spring erect and my skin tingles. Her acknowledgement has my heart pounding jubilantly in my chest as I hurry to my lecture. Suddenly, my whole world has changed. As I stride along, I puff a tune, whistling through my teeth a Beatles song: 'Help me get my feet back on the ground'.

I have a goal and my studies can take second place for a while.

My desire for Vicki is more than I can remember with any other girl.

In the days following, Vicki is often with her group, older male students, law students. Group members affect tiredness or perhaps boredom and make cynical remarks or laconic jokes. They laugh at each other and call each other by nicknames, lolling on the furniture, putting up their feet and striking poses, having a great time. I can't get close to her. I think of going boldly up to her but dismiss the idea because she seems so sophisticated, while I am so naïve.

For the first time in my life I feel out of my class. I have never before thought about a girl's social class, at least not consciously. Vicki and her group seem to be sophisticated and middle class, but it could be superficial. I can imagine myself as one of them next year. I feel the equal of Vicki on the inside, where it counts.

I wanted to meet Vicki socially. The Students' Union holds dances on Saturday nights, called 'hops', with music by popular bands. I looked for her in vain. There were plenty of girls who lived and worked in the city. They teetered around in groups on high-heeled platform-soled shoes, enjoying the music and dancing, hoping to meet the boy of their dreams. Students called these tottering girls 'totty'. I learned to call the hops 'cattle markets'. I learned that Vicki wouldn't come to a hop. She would probably be at a middle-class private party, out on a date, or at home.

On the following Monday, in the Union coffee lounge, when one of her companions vacates a seat, I sit down beside her.

'Hi,' I say. I am self-conscious, trying to hide my Yorkshire accent, saying as little as possible. 'I'm Tom.'

'Hi.' She gives me a perfunctory smile and looks away, disinterested.

I am tall and fair with the straight nose of an aristocrat, school principal or inspector of police, and high cheekbones. I am upright with a distinguished bearing. I have broad shoulders tapering to a slim waist with strong arms, thighs and legs. My movements are deliberate and powerful. I am adept at swimming, skiing and simple dances but awkward at soccer. I am unable to follow even simple routines such as aerobics and yoga.

I am dressed in a brightly coloured shirt and jeans, with large feet wearing desert boots.

I offer her a cigarette. She accepts it and I light it.

'Where are you from?' I ask her.

'Salisbury.'

'Wiltshire?'

'Yes. Not Rhodesia.'

She continues to look away. I suppose male students pester her all the time.

'Are you going to the protest?' I ask in my broad Yorkshire accent. The Students' Union was organising a rally in support of increased government grants to students.

'Maybe.'

'I will be going,' I tell her, 'though it won't make any difference to me. I'm on the minimum grant.'

She looks interested. Her face is soft and mobile but sets in a few expressions that hide what she is thinking.

'You must be rich?'

She sounds middle-middle class. I want to speak like her, hiding my accent. However, I am proud of where I come from. I have never exchanged more than a few words with a middle class girl from down south before.

'No,' I tell her. 'My parents have a bit of brass and they pay my bills.'

'Good for you,' she says.

'I like your gold things,' I say. I speak carefully with an Oxford accent, as spoken by BBC newsreaders.

'Thanks. They cheer me up.'

'Is something wrong?'

'My father is ill.'

'Is it serious?'

'Dementia'

'What do your parents do?'

She speaks hesitantly, as if the situation is tentative.

'My mother has, um, chemists' shops. My father has stopped working.'

I deduce she is middle-middle.

'I'm sorry to hear about your father. Is he bad then?'

'Pretty bad. He doesn't know who I am any more. Look, I have a lecture. I'll see you around.'

She is not a snob. She has come out of her shell and is reaching out to me as an equal.

'See you around. I'm Tom, by the way.'

'You said. I'll remember.'

'Bye, Vicki.'

She smiles and is gone.

I am besotted.

In aiming to win this girl, I know I am an outsider, with odds against me.

CHAPTER 13 LADDERS

Another way to obtain a girl friend at Birmingham University is the informal 'ladder' method. Males and females ascend an imaginary two sided step ladder, which poses the agreed ratings of males and females opposite each other. I will try to match Vicki on the ladder. The most attractive single girls are those rated highest by the male students, whereas those with least man-pulling ability are left down near the bottom. Unattached male students are rated according to female attention, getting most attention from girls near the top of the ladder. Fresher males like me are near the bottom. Although the ladders are imaginary, they all know who is on top and everyone's ranking.

When the students are all gathered together, males and females stand together in small groups of similar desirability, with their gender. There is a melee as everyone tries to assert their own value.

The final step is when a male and a female of similar desirability are aligned. The most desirable female is expected to pair off with the most desirable male, with a little flexibility for personal preferences. The second most desirable female would gladly accept the most desirable male but when he is already taken she settles for the second most desirable, again with a little flexibility. The process continues until, because there is a surplus of males, the least desirable males remain untaken and have to chase skirt off-campus or spend their time in the bar playing darts or getting drunk. When there is a surplus of unmatched girls or men, they pair off for queer social activities.

When one of them perceives the match he or she wants is above her or him, they are guided by the their perception of value from an exchange, trying to be equal. Tom is aware he is below Vicki, who is higher up. He can wait for his value to appreciate or for Vicki's value to fall.

Fresher men like me are not rated high enough up the ladder to pair off with a university girl but we will get our chance in second year. First year relationships generally don't last into second year.

Traditional matching is approximated with many variations. A minority of strange women and bizarre men are matched by high-ranked individuals. Weird pairings disrupt but do not destroy the hierarchies. Availability of The Pill has meant that men are no longer expected to take responsibility for offspring from sexual relations. Consequently, the coupling process is more for instant gratification and ratings are awarded more for fashionable qualities, such as socialism, social connections and sports cars, than for traditional values such as heredity, virginity and family support. I am looking forward to getting a pairing in second year.

I didn't form a pair with any girl in my first attempt on the ladder.

By my reckoning, the best way to get a classy chick is to get a First Class degree. Instead of spending my time on extra-curricular activities with high kudos, such as debating, I plan to hit the academic straps. I see plenty of other male students who are after the same chicks as me, withdraw from the ladder and pursue their fame in the Students' Union social venues. Who will score best in the end is going to be tested. Already a pattern is emerging.

CHAPTER 14 LOVE PAIR

Finding a girl socially on the informal ladder seems like a better plan than social climbing or studying.

One Saturday night, I am gate-crashing parties with our gang when I come across Vicki. She is dancing with her female friends. She stands out as an independent fun-loving girl with a wonderful body. I am only a little drunk and she seems pleased to see me.

'Hello, Tom.'

'Dance?'

I had the impression that Vicki would be a subdued and sedate dancer, but was delighted when she began throwing herself around vigorously, even better than Sue had in Wales.

I jived with her and danced Rock N'Roll, calypso, reggae, salsa, twist and more. She was magnificent. Onlookers watched us from the side of the room.

We showed each other our routines with feet, arms and body. She danced mechanically with a bored look on her face, as was the fashion. I try not to look awkward. When the Beatles' 'Girl' is playing, we dance close together. Her body fits perfectly against mine, and I soon become aroused. I close my eyes and imagine we are spinning endlessly in a Viennese waltz, in a magnificent ballroom. She is in a white spreading gown, with me in black tie and tails.

When the music finishes, we go out into the garden and we hold each other and talk about ourselves. She is shy and I have to prise out her personal information. As I thought, she went to an exclusive girls' school. I doubt that her classmates would go with a boy from a plebeian public grammar school like mine.

I asked her whether she had a boyfriend in first year, but she doesn't answer. I take this to mean she did. We talk about our dreams and plans, for travel and jobs. I want to be an oil tycoon. Her dreams are of travel and scholarly research. I find myself revising my plans, trying to fit in with hers. Born within a few days of each other, we are two of a kind, both dreamers. Like me, she is introverted and a little nervous in company, forcing joviality with a supercilious grin, fiddling with her hair nervously. I want to help her overcome her lack of confidence, her little-girl word clutters under the spotlight of group conversation. Most of all, I liked the way she seemed to understand me, listening to me uncritically.

We hug and her hair smells clean and her skin of flowers. Then we kiss. Her mouth is soft and tastes of sweet apricots. I try to French kiss her but when I delve with my tongue, she twists her head away.

'No,' she gasps.

We kiss some more and I grind my erection into her pelvis. I feel at a disadvantage about what to do next, as I am a virgin. Perhaps she is, too. In an earlier age she could have been called demure. I manage to get rid of my rides and drive her back to Exmouth Hall. As she doesn't ask me in, I kiss her outside. There is a sign forbidding visitors at night. She seems friendly; that is all.

'See you tomorrow, Vicki,' I say carefully.

'I expect so, Tom,' she says. 'Goodnight.'

'G'night.'

CHAPTER 15 DESIRING VICKI

I don't know where my desire for Vicki originated. Perhaps I was envious of Vicki's student middle class men friends and I imitated them in mimetic rivalry, desiring to be someone else, in pointless competition. According to philosopher Girard, that would be an ontological sickness.

'Desire is caught from another, not emerging from within', said philosopher Girard.

I realised that I was pursuing Vicki because she was popular, rather than from my own desire. There was kudos from being with the best-looking girl in second-year. Anyway, the music was too loud to talk and I didn't find out much about her.

We spent our time together kissing.

Vicki's diffidence has me on my back foot; so I don't try for a date. I don't want to have her turn me down. For several weeks after our first kiss, we spend time together and have a lot of fun. I soon take up with her where I had left off with Bridget, with long kisses and hugs, with the difference that I now had the privacy of 'pashing' with her in my room in hall. We lay on my bed while my hands caressed her back under her top. I wrote finger messages on her silky smooth back, for her to sense and interpret as letters and words.

'What does this say?' I ask her.

'T.O.U.C.H,' she says.

Her body is wonderful, with firm curves and soft recesses. She lets me go so far and then stops me.

We kiss as we hang out the windows and jeer in unison at pranksters, as officials try to maintain order, for example, when the police come to find out who put the warden's car in the lake. We kiss during food fights in the kitchen. We kiss when our gang creates a disease hoax and quarantines everyone. We kiss as we watch a beer-vomiting race. And we kiss at the formal ball.

She is lovely, a positive spirit. She looks at flowers, speaks to birds, strokes cats and pats dogs. She smiles wryly at strangers, with a suggestion of naughtiness. But when you meet her, she is trusting and open, looks levelly, shakes hands firmly, holds eye contact. She is gentle and graceful, with fine-boned legs, long skirts and hips that swing alluringly; she wears soft materials and pastel colours. On some matters such as cruelty to children and animals, she displays a campaigner's zeal and will brook no compromise.

I am delighted to find she is neither vain nor precious. She is beautiful without make-up and wears it invisibly. She is intelligent and insightful and can read my emotions like a book.

After kissing to get to know her, there is kissing to build up trust, and then kissing to undress her. Kissing and a painful bulge in the front of my jeans is all I get. I don't shag her, because I am too inexperienced. I don't take the lead because I don't have her support. I have always found myself unable to make love to a passive woman, for then it is just sex. Love has to be a shared experience, equal and lasting.

We see each other every day. To my consternation she wants to spend more and more time with the others, socialising. I blame myself for lack of sexual experience to keep her interested. It is the same with my conversation but I learn to tease out her deep thoughts. They are critical and incisive. I have never known anyone as intelligent and I learn so much from her about people, their motives and their deceptions. We go to the movies together with our group and she holds my hand. When I ask, she explains who is who, because in a complex plot, I forget who characters are.

When she takes on too much, which is often, she tends to neglect those closest to her. Her inertia, her tendency to keep doing what she is already doing, is large. Her days are filled with activities and routines she has engaged in for many years and has scheduled forward in her mind. She lacks flexibility to vary her schedule to deal with new and emerging needs. She fits me in, but it costs her a big effort to be flexible.

Unlike me, she is gregarious and hangs out in groups. Whereas some girls speak to draw attention to themselves, Vicki speaks for effect, quietly in measured tones, occasionally with explicit reflection. She is disorganised and untidy but makes an effort occasionally to create an ambitious event, such as a theme party, with others' support.

I am very happy. I am doing well in my course, and I have Vicki who is wonderful. I have surprised myself that I have as my girlfriend the best-looking girl on campus. Since I first saw her in the Students' Union coffee lounge, she has been at the centre of my life. I have gone full circle from wanting independence when I was with Bridget, to waiting for Vicki to settle down with me.

Our relationship doesn't settle down and it doesn't seem to be going anywhere. Vicki is transactional and the transactions stop. Vicki no longer comes to my room. Empathy is not my forté, but I have the idea that Vicki won't have sex with me because I am a virgin. It is a Catch-22 situation. Vicki will not put out until I have experienced a commitment, but I will not make a commitment until Vicki has put out. It is a standoff.

We separated for the university vacation and I went to a vacation job in Montreal, Canada. Vicki went to a vacation job in psychology at North Carolina, USA. We arranged to meet up afterwards and when I arrived at her workplace, she and a girlfriend were expecting me.

'Welcome to the Lie Detection laboratory,' Vicki said.

'What type of lie detection?' I asked.

'Here they investigate methods of interrogating suspects for the FBI and CIA.'

'Blimey.'

'Would you like to be tested?' she asked.

She wanted it and I volunteered.

The staff strapped me in a dentist's chair and covered me with electrodes.

'The electrodes measure skin resistance. If you lie, perspiration will reduce skin resistance and be recorded on these charts.'

Then they asked me questions over headphones. When the questions became intimate, I was embarrassed and tried to get up, but I couldn't move.

'Relax, we'll be finished soon.'

For 30 minutes the questions explored my sex life, including my activities with Vicki and my other girlfriends, in great detail, who I liked most and so on. It included details of what I did by myself. My answers showed I was besotted with Vicki and that was no secret.

The questioning had been intrusive and I resented it. The exposure of my feelings for Vicki had clearly been contrived by her and put me at a disadvantage that was a stumbling block in our relationship. It was a low-point in our relationship so far. I supposed that her asking about my other girlfriends was a test of loyalty and could be grounds for disaffection.

I regretted that I had volunteered.

CHAPTER 16 SOCIAL CLASS

Finding a suitable girl had considerations beyond matching of desire and establishing a relationship. Traditionalists wanted a match of social classes too.

I was born into farming stock, but I wanted to shed my provincial, rural, farm tenant, lower-middle class identity, to be more middle class like Vicki.

Brits tend to classify a person by the way he or she speaks. George Bernhard Shaw, in his play, 'Pygmalion', tested having a lower class girl pass as upper class, after education in speech. Her unfashionable vocabulary and tortured pronunciation were incongruous. Education was said to be a great leveler, a better indicator than breeding. A Labour politician said:

'At university, an aristocrat and the son of a coal miner can rub shoulders.'

This was the thesis in DH Lawrence's 'Lady Chatterley's Lover', with an unbridgeable chasm between her upper classness and a well-born but educationally and socially deprived gamekeeper, Mellors, stuck in the working class. They both have birth, brains and intimacy, but the game-keeper's education is rudimentary. It was a tryst between nature and nurture. It seemed idealistic.

For a marriage match, both nature and nurture could be considered. Jane Austen put love above both in 'Pride and Prejudice'. Although education, skills and social connections are ascendant under American influence, heredity nevertheless persisted of great importance in the UK. Whereas in America wealth is a class of its own, in Britain class cannot be bought. 'Old money' is required for entry to the upper class and is often frozen in hereditary assets. Because 'new' money is more available for luxury cars and yachts, to the impoverished upper class such items are sour grapes, in 'bad taste', bourgeois and vulgar.

Even new money could be acceptable in the UK. Jane Austen wrote 'It is a truth universally acknowledged, that a single man in possession of a good fortune, must be in want of a wife.'

Like most of my peers, I did not possess a good fortune and would have to obtain a wife on the strength of other qualities. Each class has distinct occupations, habitats, ownership, possessions, education, behaviors, languages, customs, recreations and entertainments. The subspecies, 'Farmer', can vary from lower class, at the level of a subsistence farm with a cottage plot and a few animals, to middle class where the owner is the partner operating a food production conglomerate with intensive meat-growing factories and robotic dairying. Somewhere along this spectrum, were tenant farmers like the Archers.

'We are working class,' my mother said, exuding hubris as she waited to be corrected that as an employer of workers, my father could not be working class.

Tenant farmers are somewhere between working and middle class. They do not have the independent income of the professional, military and clergy, or the investment income of land and property owners. They work for themselves in a secure occupation and this puts them a cut above the wage-earning laboring classes.

Vicki seemed to be middle-middle. She spoke plummy BBC English, was demure and good-humoured and went to a private school for girls. It must have been a school for middle class girls, because she had a wider understanding of cultured life than I did. She drove a new car and holidayed on the Continent, off the beaten track. She shopped at Selfridges, Debenhams and Waitrose, but not with aristocrats and the nouveau riches at Harrods. Vicki used to sail on her father's yacht. She no longer goes to church, but takes an interest in politics and goes to the theatre regularly. I haven't asked Vicki about her ancestry. If it were high class, she probably wouldn't be at a redbrick uni and would probably be in a job where she would meet high-class males, such as arts, fashion or publishing.

Engineering students in my year often have similar social classes and sometimes joined social groups from places related geographically. Middle class students can afford to live in residential halls, whereas working class students live in digs. One social group of working class students is from northeast England. Other groups include the Iraqis, the Europeans and the Colonials. A counterculture group hangs out in the Union playing snooker instead of going to lectures.

I try to join a middle-middle class group, dominated by ex-public schoolboys, involved in rugby and cricket-playing, from 'county' professional homes in the southeast. They drove sports cars in rallies at weekends. I quickly find out they didn't want me.

'Tom, as you don't have a sports car, you can stay and keep time when we cross the finish line.'

They left me stranded when they forgot to tell me which pub they were gathering at.

Next I fell in with several provincial lower middle class grammar school types like myself, led by an impoverished middle-middle class ex-public schoolboy. Our provincial dialects are revealed by his BBC English. My Yorkshire identity amuses them as much as it embarrasses me. They make me say, 'Eee lad, tha'll zoon be olt'nuff t'go down't pit' (meaning 'Well, boy, you will soon be old enough to go underground mining').

By the end of the first year, my provincial identity is preventing me from mixing with some students with whom I am planning to move into hall. At the start of second year, I decide to redefine myself as middle-middle class. This is a bold plan because one's social class normally doesn't change. However, becoming more like Vicki is highly desirable. Although opposites are sometimes said to attract, it is also said the effect does not last. On the other hand, there is little evidence that couples from different social classes complement each other. Matches of like with like are said to be most resilient. Accordingly, I become middle-middle, like Vicki, desert my former friends and fall in with Vicki's girlfriends when they start to hang around with us. As a rural provincial, I am something of a curiosity but I am not lampooned as I was in first year.

CHAPTER 17 THE GAME

I felt vulnerable with Vicki and it might be more than the difference of social class between us. I looked in some psychology books that offered advice on gender relations.

In tennis and in contract bridge, you are vulnerable when you are about to win precariously, as if on a precipice. In dating, being vulnerable was not good, a weak position. Neil Strauss' book 'The Game' documents tips and tricks to use for finding and picking up women. Men can seek women based on a deceptive ploys used by a community of secretive pick-up artists (PUAs). The book has been disparaged as misogynistic and not relevant to respectable women. I have mentioned it here as a curiosity and to embolden men to ignore their own shortcomings and adopt strategies I used as a fringe pick-up artist.

While researching his book, Neil changes from a shy, timid man and becomes an heroic pick-up artist on a world stage. He begins as insecure and awkward but, through practice, becomes one of the world's top PUAs

Many men approach women and tell them they're beautiful, whereas PUAs will speak to every woman except the one they want to pick-up. She might feel she has offended him and try to establish contact. A pick up artist could say something to lower the woman's self esteem, such as remarking her hair looks a bit funny, or she has a piece of fluff on her jacket. By such a put down, called a 'neg', the PUA makes himself more desirable. Invariably the 'negged' girl would try to win approval from the gamester, as if this would cancel the 'neg'.

Approaching women in a bar should never be straight on, nor from behind because that's intimidating and scary. Approaching at 45° is appropriate and not too confrontational. After the approach the

PUA can show he has value, by providing the woman he wants with something. He can show her a magic trick, or leave her with the impression that he is knowledgeable and valuable.

What was most intriguing however, was the PUA's manipulation of human psychology and social dynamics to influence the behaviour of the women. These worked like a type of forbidden black magic, using deception and misdirection to persuade women to give their phone numbers (and sometimes much more) to strange, wildly-dressed men they just met in a Los Angeles nightclub.

A great way to break the ice with women is to fake personality assessment, as if by an expert. Women love to talk about themselves and what they want in life.

Independently of Strauss' advice, I have used Briggs Myer Personality Assessment to gain women's interest in the four dimensions: intraversion, sensing, thinking and perceiving. Each dimension is binary and there are 16 personality types, all having definite positive attributes.

A different ploy I investigated was to comment on any difference in dilation between their eyes, which I attributed to differences in left brain and right brain thinking, with the eye on the side with most brain activity distended or bloodshot. My method hasn't been published but I have credible evidence of its utility. Girls will believe a personality rating delivered with the intimacy of expert gazing into eyes.

Deceptions are easiest in the noise, hype and romance of a night club. Some can be used outside the nightclub. They centre around manipulating assumptions and asserting social dominance over individuals to manipulate them onto paths of their choosing.

Neil describes bizarre tactics, particularly the practice of 'peacocking,' where the men wear the loudest most obnoxious articles of clothing they can find (such as large red cowboy hats and even T-shirts with light up programmable LED messages) to stand out and attract a mate, not unlike the elaborately feathered bird. A different ploy is to ask a woman to sit in a corner and talk with him, gaining prominence.

Many of these tactics could be used outside the nightclub. They centre around asserting social dominance that manipulates the woman onto paths of their choosing. Some of it gets a little goofy and delves into creepy things like hypnotism, but some of it actually seems plausible and plays off the default settings of our basic tribal mentalities.

Women are wired to find dominant men attractive. A neg makes men more desirable. Nice guys watch from the sidelines as dominant men succeed. Nice guys like me finish last.

I quickly discovered that relationships manipulated by these techniques were unsustainable and emotionally hollow. Relationships should be authentic, with self-acceptance as the basis of connection.

CHAPTER 18 SAILING WITH MARIA

Once I encountered a girl by chance who could become a partner when circumstances threw us together. Part of the story appears in my novel $hort of Love.

I was sitting in the cockpit of Ermelo, a 38-foot sloop going to Trinidad. There were seven of us aboard, all in our twenties. One was a Brazilian girl travelling the World, the others were South African or English men who had crewed during the Cape Town to Rio yacht race. I was 24 and had been offered a crewing job taking the place of someone who had flown home. It was my first time on an ocean-going sloop.

Maria had flown from Johannesburg for Carnival. Her usual job was casino croupier. She wanted to yacht-hop to exotic places. She was young and lithe with a gamin physique, skin the colour of white tea, a mop of curly black hair, very white teeth, a broad smile and an attractive face. She was wearing tight-fitting jeans and a figure hugging T-shirt. Her face had Caucasian and Negroid elements. She was vivacious and fun.

The others were sitting in the cockpit, watching the Sun go down behind the hills. They were telling jokes about the race they had finished the day before. I felt like an outsider. Bryce was sitting next to Maria.

'Where are you going to sleep, Greg?' Alan asks.

Greg looks at Bryce the skipper for an answer.

'He'll have to take Bruce's bunk,' Bryce says. Bruce had flown home to look after some business. I learned later from Greg that he had been sharing the master's cabin with Bryce, but he is now being ejected for Maria to sleep in there, because Bryce wants her.

'Is that okay, Greg?' Bryce asks politely.

'I suppose. But I wouldn't like to be Maria!'

There is a pindrop silence.

'What do you mean, Greg?' asks Bryce, taken aback.

'Your snoring!' says Greg.

Everyone laughs and looks at Maria.

'If she can't take it, I might have to put her ashore,' Bryce threatens. It doesn't seem as if it is his snoring she has to take, but Maria gamely tries to ignore his threat.

'Well, It can't be too bad or you would have moved out already, Greg,' she says. 'Can anyone tell me if you can hear it in the crew quarters?' Maria laughs nervously and looks around. No-one answered her.

The master's cabin is behind the cockpit. I figure out she is sounding us out as to whether we will be able to hear her if she screams in the cabin. It is another matter whether any crew will come to her aid.

I catch her eye and give her a small nod to show I approve of her caution. Perhaps because I am a newcomer, too, I feel an obligation to look after her.

'No, not so far,' says Alan laughing. 'But if we do hear anything we'll be pretty pissed off. The Skipper may have privileges but they don't include robbing us of our beauty sleep.' Bryce shows little interest in Maria's concern.

'It will take more than sleep to make you beautiful, Alan,' quips Bryce, changing the subject.

Maybe Alan, too, would help her. I can see the other two wouldn't go against Bryce. He looks and talks tough like a skipper, and his stories about policing show he is a physical man. He is a Boer and fiercely proud of white ascendency and the apartheid system. His views are very different from mine, but I respect his right to air them on his own boat. I will not confront him, unless he is directly affecting me or those I care for.

I play on my guitar Dylan's 'The Times They Are A-changing'. They listen unmoved, not being sympathetic to the youth revolution. So next I bash out 'Michael Row the Boat Ashore' and they join in lustily. When I get to 'Sister help to trim the sail', Bryce interrupts me.

'Do you know 'Sloop John B'?'

I arpeggio the chords, singing falsetto, and they all join in on the chorus.

We sing for another hour and then I turn in. Maria goes ashore for the night. My hammock is in the damp and smelly forward cabin.

In the morning Maria brings her stuff on board.

'We will sail after lunch,' Bryce announces.

The morning is spent in a flurry of activity as all the crew help prepare the yacht. We take out all the sails, dry them in the Sun, fold them carefully and stow them in the sail locker with the eyes of the sails uppermost ready to be cleated and lofted. We fill the water tanks, and disinfect the head and galley. We fill our tanks with water and stow the food and booze brought by Bryce. Then we wash the decks and take our last showers in the clubhouse.

When everything is shipshape we bring in the mooring lines and motor out of Guanabara Bay, putting up the sails as we go. Bryce turns off the motor. The only sounds are the slosh from our bow wave, with gurgles from the keel and the creak of taut sheets as with the wind abeam we reach northwards. We all sit in a line with our legs outboard along the starboard gunwale, watching Corcovado Peak with the white statue of Christ, arms outstretched, slowly sinking from view. This is an adventure I wouldn't miss for quids.

As the Sun dives down, Rio glows on the horizon. We have sundowners of a tot of rum apiece in the cockpit. Bryce's singing is terrible, but no-one tells him to stop. Greg in the galley passes up to us in the cockpit plates of pies and beans. We drink more rum. Gradually, the guys disappear below to their bunks, leaving just Alan, Bryce and me with Maria. Bryce tries to put his arm around her but she moves away. I keep the chat going, to give time for Bryce to sober up, but eventually he tells her that she has to turn in now, so as not to come down later and disturb him. Alan and I take the watch to midnight.

It is mid-morning when Maria appears, with a black eye. When Bryce goes below for a minute, she crosses the cockpit and sits beside me. She whispers, 'He hit me. Unless I have sex with him he's going to put me ashore in Recife. I don't have any money.'

At sundown, Bryce regales us with stories of how he implemented the apartheid laws in his police job, brutalizing black men and black women. Maria is terrified. She is part negro and afraid of the monstrous Bryce. The other guys seem to think he is acceptable. They are inured to the racism of the police in South Africa. Bryce tells story after story of his bigotry until I can stand it no more and turn in.

Next day, I am having breakfast in the cockpit when Bryce comes up. There is no sign of Maria and I assume she is too frightened to appear.

'How are you getting along?' Bryce asks me, as if being aware of my presence for the first time.

'Maria told me you hit her,' I say fiercely. 'When I get off this boat I will seek an International Citizens Arrest Warrant from the International Common Law Court of Justice.'

Bryce is taken aback. 'It was an accident,' he answers. 'You need to keep focussed on your sailing or you might never get to where you want to go. It can get pretty rough out here. Accidents happen. We're in international waters. There's no law out here and people can do what they like.'

It is an ugly threat. She is in danger, and so am I, if I try to help her.

'She has human rights and International Court Law applies,' I tell him. 'She is not going to sleep in your cabin anymore. You keep your hands off her. She'll sleep in the crews' bunks when they're on shift.'

'So what will happen when they come off shift?'

'She'll change to another bunk.'

'You're kidding! Would you kick her out? No way. You'll climb in beside her. You want her, don't you? Why should she be with you when it's my boat? She'll have to sleep in the bow locker, with the door closed so the guys can get some privacy changing their gear.'

The locker is a cupboard.

'It's full of gear. There's no ventilation.'

'The door is slatted and she can sleep on top of the sail bags. I'm not having her take the crew's minds off their jobs. She'll soon come back to my cabin. You'll see.'

While we were talking Maria came up and heard this proposal.

'What do you want to do, Maria?' I ask her. 'Will you sleep in the sail locker?'

Maria nods.

I say to her, 'Is that okay?'

She nods, relieved.

'You can have the black bitch,' Bryce says, getting up, 'until we get to Recife.'

Our watch, Alan and me, take on Maria. We are on from midnight to 8.00am, and the watch ends when we get breakfast for everyone. She stays with us, learning how to steer a compass course, trim the sails and help in a sail change.

I love sailing, travelling as free as the wind. A sailing boat has to be rigged carefully and continually adjusted for maximum efficiency.

On Ermelo, so far I had learned that there are decent people who will stand up against evil if they are led. Derrida's deconstruction of the situation could have concluded that mixed gender groups of strangers are unstable at close quarters, but a leader who is a tyrant will be opposed.

CHAPTER 19 OIL SLICK

Shortly after leaving Rio, we were caught in a storm and blown halfway to Africa. When the wind subsided, we turned and headed back. We had no radio and navigated by sextant, finding Recife in northern Brazil partly by chance.

We anchored a couple of kilometres from shore because Recife bay was shallow. We were hungry, bruised and beaten by the huge waves that battered us and it was everyone's idea to have a shower and find some fresh food.

All seven of us squeezed into the ship's dinghy. Alan, our best oarsman, rowed us into Recife Yacht Club. Maria brought her pack to take with her but Bryce told her there wasn't enough room in the dinghy for it and he would put her ashore tomorrow. She had kept out of his way, and he seemed to be backing down on wanting her to leave. She is well-liked by the crew and has made herself useful. If he makes her go now, he will be unpopular.

We have lunch at the club. Then we help Bryce carry supplies down to the dinghy from the supermarket over the road. Most of it is cans of beer. I can't believe everything will fit in, but we sit on the supplies with about two centimetres of freeboard.

'Steady! You'll have us in the water!' Bryce warned Alan.

We are quite drunk and we sing at the top of our voices. I organise us to sing in three parts: 'Row, row, row your boat.' We are making a lot of noise and laughing. When we are about halfway back, we see a wave breaking continuously, pouring water down as if in slow motion, like a bore, but the bay is wide and open to the sea. No-one has seen this phenomenon before, and we are mesmerised.

'Let's get a closer look,' I say.

Alan is rowing us towards it when suddenly, from under a flat sea, a wave rears up and dumps us. The dinghy turns over, and before we can grab it, it is carried away on a breaking wave, leaving us in the water surrounded by groceries with bobbing cans of beer. The shore is about a kilometre away. It will be a demanding swim.

Without a word, the guys set off swimming for the shore. I start to follow when I hear Maria call faintly.

'Help! I can't swim!'

She is clinging to an oar, trying to keep her head above water. I swim over to her and put her in a lifesaving position, floating on her back with her head on my chest. I tell myself not to have sexual designs on this girl. I feel privileged to be able to help her.

'Thank you,' she says.

I begin backstroking with one arm and kicking steadily, with the experience of one lifesaving lesson in my school's pool. It is a long way but I will be able to take rests.

I wonder for a moment why it has fallen to me to take her in alone. I suppose the other guys' swimming may not be good, or maybe they are too drunk to care for anyone except themselves.

I change my backstroke to the other arm for a while, and then back again.

I am getting tired. I get Maria to hold on to my shoulders in front, with her body under me as I swim breaststroke. It is slower but easier. I ask her to kick to help me. Having her lithe body moving under me is exciting and I want her. I think she feels me against her. She smiles at me. I look away to hide my embarrassment.

There is a shout from ahead, and I tread water to see. There are several hours of daylight left. One of the guys is waving to me, pointing along the shore to the right.

'Oil,' he shouts. 'Go around.'

Just our luck. I turn and follow him parallel to the shore. But I am tired and I am having difficulty, coughing to clear water from my lungs. He shows no sign of turning in towards the shore. I'm desperate, thinking I might not make it. I turn and head for the closest shore and swim into the slick. My arms are coated with black goo, and there is an oily taste in my mouth. The oil becomes thick and heavy, with globs sticking to Maria's hair. I curse whoever spilled it. It gets into my eyes and they become bleary. I take my direction from the Sun. My limbs are so heavy I can hardly move them. Just when I am thinking I have had it, a wave lifts us, then another and another. Maria is torn out of my grip and we are dumped by a breaker. She disappears and I swim in a circle frantically. My foot touches her and I pull her up to the surface, both of us coughing weakly. Then my foot touches the beach and I first walk, then crawl, hauling her up onto the sand, where I collapse, exhausted.

The others come and look at us. We are covered with black filth. They find it funny.

'They won't let you into the yacht club like that,' says Bryce.

Because I know he is a racist bastard, I think it is a racist comment.

'Or you into the life-saving club,' I say.

'Aren't we the big hero?' he sneers. 'One guess who gets into her hammock tonight.'

Maria looks at him but says nothing.

We walk along to the sailing club and the guys all go in. They have no oil on them. Maria stays outside with me. Alan comes out with a couple of buckets, some rags, a bar of soap and a bottle of diesel.

'Diesel? Hell! Don't they have any liquid detergent or turps?' I ask.

'Sorry, it's all they have.'

I had used diesel on the farm to clean my hands and arms after working on engines. It isn't much good as a skin cleaner – too oily – but better than nothing. My skin hurts. It is sunburnt through my T-shirt from sailing under the noonday sun at the Equator. There is no shade near the tap. Now I have to suffer the stinging diesel as we fry in full sun while trying to clean up. By the time I am reasonably clean, I am feeling pinpricks all over my skin. I felt nauseous with a throbbing headache. Maria seemed to be okay. Her dark skin wasn't sunburnt like mine.

Bryce buys more groceries, and a local yachtie takes us all out to Ermelo in his runabout. Maria collects her things and goes ashore with him. She is going to Sao Paolo for a visit with her family. I lend her $30 for the bus fare; she will send it to me in England.

'Thank you for saving me,' she says simply. With a hug, she is gone, with all her belongings in a kitbag over her shoulder. She leaves a piece of paper in my hand. It is her addresses, in Brazil and South Africa. I feel like I did with Vicki after the lie detector, as if there is nothing more I can do at present. If something is meant to happen between us, it will.

By the time we clear the headland, I am alternately vomiting and lying in my bunk in a pool of sweat. My head is thumping, and I take some aspirin. I want to shit but I have been constipated ever since boarding Ermelo a week previously. Alan tells me boats affect some people that way.

Next morning, everything is fuzzy and distant. I become delirious and do not know where I am. Alan takes my temperature and it is dangerously high. Bryce shows no concern.

He comes up to my bunk and looks at me.

'We can't get a doctor out here,' he says. 'We're beyond radio contact.'

'Can we go back in?' asks Alan.

'Not for this useless hippy,' Bryce says. He must have looked in my pack and seen my bandanas and love beads. 'If he dies, we'll slip him over the side, when the others are asleep and no-one will be any the wiser.'

'You can't do that!' exclaims Alan. Of all the crew, he was the friendliest.

'Just watch me,' Bryce says.

Bryce's hammock-side visit does nothing to lift my spirits. Fortunately, Alan recognises I am dehydrated and makes me drink mug after mug of water and bathes me with a cool wet sponge.

After about four days I begin to feel better. I lurch up to the cockpit for sundowners. They give me a big hand.

'That's the best imitation of dying I've ever seen,' says Bryce callously. His compliments always have a sting.

'With all that diesel in you, watch out your farts don't ignite,' someone jokes.

'Ha ha.'

'Have you had a shit yet?' asks Alan.

'Yes.'

'Alleluia!'

It is glorious to feel well and sit in the cockpit as we rollick along to the West Indies on a broad beam reach. The conventional wisdom is, 'A woman on board causes trouble' but Maria had fitted in well. I wondered when I would see her again. The difficulties we had shared were a bond between us .

Philosopher Derrida could have concluded that care for crew members who are vulnerable can be limited when they are strangers and have to compete for their safety. Protection of disadvantaged group members can entail self-sacrifice.

CHAPTER 20 CLASS DIFFERENCES

Vicki and I were still friends but the love affair when we first met had fizzled. To my chagrin. There had been several times when I thought we would get together but it hadn't happened. Vicki had snubbed me, by going with me to a ball but spending the evening flirting with locals and I was hurt. I felt I was the wrong social class for her. In the UK, social class is established by what school you went to, by old money and by breeding. I had learned to fake them. I got no pleasure from misleading superficial enquirers and felt no guilt in that enterprise. But she had not accepted me.

I had adopted a new social class which morphed into Vicki's. To make my social identity more acceptable, first I distanced myself from my family and former class peers by absenting myself from their company. I learned to speak Oxford English, deserting my Somerset lowlands garble, which advertised my uncouth lack of intelligence and culture.

I tried to climb up to Vicki's class by acquiring her speech, conversation, colloquialisms, slang, swearing, values, attitudes, materials, locales, experiences and media interests. I learned to mimic a range of regional accents and postures, within which I could hide my Somerset accent. I soon had a repertoire of comic dialects that I used to showcase the neutral speech I was developing. I could conceal my new identity with Somerset, Yorkshire, London, Devon and Texan accents.

Imitating Vicki's bourgeois BBC English was difficult and dangerous if I was found out. Working class lingo revealed I was a prole.

I admired Vicki so much, I would happily end my search for love and sex in a relationship with her. However, I realized that it would take some time to develop a relationship and that early sex with her was unlikely, whatever commitment I made. The major obstacle between Vicki and me could be our different customs for exclusive relationships, which I didn't understand. If I pursued another girl, I would do so openly. Yorkshire people take pride in straight dealing and straight talking, at the risk of bluntness and terseness. A Wortham girl would never have deserted me at the May Ball in Cambridge the way Vicki did.

By contrast, we find southerners insincere, devious and reticent to call a spade a spade. I fear that Vicki may be a 'prick teaser' who enjoys keeping me, as well other guys, on a piece of string, to haul us in when she wants us. I didn't have time for that and would sniff around for a girl who was more accommodating.

Bright, adventurous and beautiful, Vicki stands very high in my female hierarchy. I am making it my business to claw my way up the male ladder as high as hard work can get me. Without class as a barrier between us, she was my ideal match.

CHAPTER 21 COMMODITY MARKETS

I was infatuated with, but frustrated by, Vicki. The supposed pairing off between gender hierarchies wasn't working for me. Vicki seemed to be higher up than I could ever reach and I was disillusioned. The uncertainty and emotional cost was more than I could afford.

'Ladder matching couples is superficial, corruptible and unreliable,' I thought. *'There has to be a better way to find a partner.'*

I was interested in methods for matching buyers and sellers where prices varied in time with supply and demand. I was writing an assignment on the commodification of crude oil. It seemed likely a global oil futures market would be established soon.

'What is good for trading crude oil, might possibly be good for trading love,' I thought.

I wondered if a commodity market could trade love prospects as commodities. There was demand, supply, substitution and matching of buyers and sellers. Men and women could have wider choices than under the system prevailing at LUT, with its ranking of males and females and pairing off from the top.

'Oils ain't oils,' was the objection of suppliers of the best quality crude oils used for gasoline.

'We can crack anything,' was the mantra of refinery engineers who bought low quality oils cheaply.

'You get what you pay for,' was the credo of brokers who arranged trades. For the first time in history, oil was being dealt with as a commodity, a tradable product. I was convinced by my study that trading of futures in oil would stabilise prices and enable suppliers and refiners to get on with their work without oil supply uncertainty. Perhaps love could be traded between buyers and sellers.

'Love matches at present lack the rigour that could be obtained if love was dealt with as a commodity. Traditional matching is inferior. Girls ain't girls.'

A woman would have full rights of self-determination and would give her consent to a relationship before any trade took place.

'If love was a commodity, I could do a trade and get on with my work,' I thought.

I complained about my frustration with Vicki to Larry. Lisa was there.

'What do you want from a girl? A life partnership?' Larry asked.

'No,' I said.

'A girl wants a man who will commit to settling down,' Lisa told me. She and Larry had become inseparable. 'Do you think you'll ever want to settle down with a steady girlfriend, Tom?'

'No. Getting hitched won't be on my agenda until I'm thirty.'

'Could there be a girl who changes your mind?'

'I doubt it. She would have to be special!'

'Would you like to meet my friend Barbara?' Lisa asked.

I hesitated for a moment, wondering how Vicki would react in competition with Barbara. But Vicki hadn't shown much interest in me for weeks. A problem is that the customs of her class lead her to expect that a guy should pursue her exclusively, whereas at home we do not expect a guy and a girl to become exclusive until they are engaged. To have an exclusive relationship with Vicki, I was prepared to get engaged and looked for an opportunity to obtain rights over her. But this had been the situation with Vicki for months. I wasn't getting anywhere. I was used to finding my girlfriends myself but I hadn't been successful for some time and it was time to move on.

'Okay,' I told Lisa doubtfully.

Lisa gave me a phone number and I called and made a date.

Later that week my battered old car pulled up in front of a tidy detached house in a suburb near the university. I knocked at the front door.

'I'm Barbara.' She held out a fine hand.

'Tom. Pleased to meet you.'

Her hand was delicate. I opened a car door for her. She was slim and rather angular with a shy face that came alive when she smiled.

We went to a pub and talked over drinks. She was intelligent but under-confident and I liked her. She worked as a secretary.

'My grades weren't good enough to go to university,' she said sadly.

I was embarrassed that my own success had probably been unfair.

'Why weren't your grades higher?' I asked.

'I didn't try hard enough. There was no encouragement. No-one expected me to go to university.'

'Girls are treated unfairly,' I said. 'Perhaps you will be a big success at something else.'

'I'm trying. Do you think I'm dumb because I don't go to university?'

I didn't, but the difference in our activities was difficult to ignore. I spent most of my time studying, while Barbara worked office hours and then spent her time with nothing to show for it. I didn't meet her friends and I seemed to exist in a separate compartment of her life where our interaction revolved around having sex.

It was an arrangement that suited me well, but it was not my idea of a trade in a market for love. Commodification of love could arouse suspicion that the intent was for men and women to exploit each other.

Trading in love would have to protect women from exploitation, benefitting them without any possibility of harm. I knew that money in love transactions could arouse fear of sexual slavery and human trafficking. Sexual slavery and trafficking in women were illegal. It was unlawful to abduct, hold captive, apply force to, sexually assault, exploit sexually, bigamise, or psychologically harm any person.

Trading in a love market would be by mutual consent. I felt sure I could devise market regulations that would prevent non-consensual trading, in the same way that deception, fraud, theft and other hazards were prevented in oil trading. I was determined to turn my experience into a love market.

Compared with the ladder matching method, a love market would allow everyone to participate and would not depend on social appraisal and covert ratings of arbitrary value by an 'in crowd'. Buyers and sellers needed to be aware of many exchanges occurring and be able to value offers realistically.

I was convinced a well-organised love market could attract speculators and improve love matching. It would replace complex and inequitable negotiations between men and women with structured exchange such as between wheat growers and millers about quality. The presence of speculators would stabilise the market and benefit everyone.

A person seeking a love partner could want a match immediately, or search carefully online until they eventually found someone to meet their needs. A person's attractiveness could increase or decrease with age, experience and presentation skills. Their wants could change and so the finding of a partner required diligence and luck. The love market had to prevent deception and abuse.

'To advertise my new method I can get drama students to put on a spoof ridiculing current matching difficulties,' I thought. 'First I need to develop the terms of agreement.'

I talked with a LUT researcher who was trialling a computer dating service but there was little transparency and no role for speculators. Genuine lovers insisted on transparency. The love market, as it existed in computer dating, was not transparent. Buyers and sellers were self-promoting, not explicitly declaring their assets and often intending to deceive. This was a make-believe world and could result in fraud, exploitation, emotional hurt and disappointment.

I lacked practical commodity market experience. I could not start a love-trading enterprise until I had more experience and could demonstrate a relationship with a female with whom I had traded love successfully. My relationship with Barbara had love but seemed incomplete because she seemed reticent to offer herself in a trade with another mand. She stuck to me and I could see that finishing with her was a problem I would have to solve soon.

Unable to secure love with Vicki, I had a love relationship with Barbara.

CHAPTER 22 COMMODITY SPECULATION

A computer dating service started at the university and I was curious whether I could start a dating system that would match men and women as efficiently as buyers and sellers of oil were finding each other on the commodity exchange.

I met Wilbur, an American researcher at LUT, who paid for his sports car and skiing holidays with his profits from speculating on commodities.

'When commodities compete, how does that work?' I asked him.
'You mean when they are substitutes for each other?'
'Yes.'
'A buyer gets various offers,' Wilbur said.
'Different prices for the same thing?'
'Similar things. He would look for the cheapest offer.'
'Like a sailor with a girl in every port?' I said.
'The quality of a commodity can vary. A sailor would be selective.'
'Would their prices differ?'
'The prices of substitutes would vary with quality.'
'Also with supply and demand?' I asked.
'Yes. There would be more girls in some ports than in others.'
'Prices might be lower where there is poverty, I suppose,' I said.
'Markets are never perfect. Prices he would pay in different ports would relate to prices of substitutes.'
'So prices for commodities are always relative?'
'Yes. My experience is with grains: wheat, barley, oats — that sort of thing,' said Wilbur. 'The prices are relative because they can substitute for each other.'
'Do the different grains have steady prices?'

'They do from week to week but not from year to year,' Wilbur said. 'Grain trades involve physical supplies and demands.'

'Love can get pretty physical,' I said, pretending experience.

'Love has an emotional component too,' he said.

'I suppose hungry people get emotional about grains,' I said.

'The demand for grains is for future delivery from storage. Love is more spontaneous and immediate.'

'Not always,' I replied. 'There can be a waiting time until delivery, called engagement.'

'Hmm. I suppose a love commitment could be like a 'future',' Wilbur said.

'Could I make an investment to trade a girl like a commodity?'

'You can't be serious!'

'I am. Why not?'

'What a hoot! You will be in big trouble when the girl finds out. Every girl thinks she is unique, with a mystical quality that Mister Right will appreciate when she finds him.'

'Isn't each grain shipment unique?'

'Yes — the price is adjusted for quality,' said Wilbur. 'Grains have price adjustments for high and low quality. But it is not the same as valuing a girl's unique quality. There is no formula for adjusting a girl's price. Dating services are paid for by both men and women, each wanting to connect with a person they could have affection for during correspondence or in a meeting. The problem is that people exaggerate, lie and try to put one over on other applicants. I'm not saying it won't be possible to trade a girl as a commodity, but that each buyer would appreciate each girl differently, not as a predictable commodity.'

'Trades could be individuated.'

'Exactly,' said Wilbur. 'Would you like to see how commodity trading works by investing in a grains straddle? You will see that commodity trades are individuated, but the adjustments to prices are universal and honest, preventing disappointment. The economic dimension is the most important and final. Agreement is reached at a certain price.'

'I doubt a girl could be traded like that. Price could come first, with adjustment later.'

'That would be different. You would have to try it and see. I have an awesome prospect in grain trading for you. You are sure to double your money. Are you interested?'

'That sounds great.'

'It's a spread. I'll explain.'

CHAPTER 23 GRAIN SPREAD

Wilbur thought that the love market I was proposing could be unethical, but he helped me to understand how it could work.
'What do you mean by 'a spread?'' I asked.
'A spread is between two different commodities, often called an inter-commodity spread. It involves taking simultaneous long and short positions in the futures markets of two related commodities. This approach aims to profit from changes in the price difference (spread) between the two commodities, rather than their absolute price levels.'
'Could I have a spread on girls?'
'What girls?' he asked.
'Two types: girl graduates and girl secretaries.'
'Vickis and Barbaras? If they were wheat and barley, you might buy wheat expecting it to increase and sell barley expecting it to fall. You would have protection and profit from the difference. The trader buys (goes long) in a contract in one commodity and sells (goes short) in a contract on a related commodity at the same time and for the same delivery month. Profit or loss depends on how the price difference, or spread, changes—not on price changes for either commodity alone.'
'How much profit??'
'You would deposit three thousand dollars minimum for each trade. Imagine three thousand dollars is the cost of buying a railcar of wheat and you can spend an equal amount of money buying a railcar of barley to cover the short you would sell. A deposit of $6000 for the spread'
'$6000 is a lot of money compared with the cost of my room in hall, which is $100 dollars per week. I could borrow it until

September from my father's overdraft account. I'll have to pay it back by September.'

That was when my father had to pay the rent for the farm.

'No worries. By then you will have made a large profit.'

'How sure are you?'

'It's a cinch. Wheat and barley prices have never been as close as they are now. When the gap widens back to normal, you will profit big-time. These trades will be made at a margin of 5%, meaning your profits and losses on nominal amounts will be multiplied by 20.'

'Who is putting up the 95%?'

'The broker, for a fee,' Wilbur said. 'Delivery is not until the end of September. That's why they call it a 'future'. If grain crops are destroyed by bad weather in Russia, the USA or Canada, the wheat price will increase and offset your extra cost of buying scarce barley if its price increases too. You will be protected.'

'What if wheat falls?'

'Barley's price is likely to fall too and your loss will be balanced with your short protecting you.'

'Am I exposed to the difference between the two commodities, with a spread between them.'

'Exactly. Sometimes the gap isn't normal and you can lose.'

'How can a gap be normal?' I asked.

'When it narrows to the usual gap again.'

'Yes. The gap between wheat and barley is narrower today than at any time in the past twenty years — without good reason. If a new animal feed technology had been invented that favours substitution of barley, the gap could narrow permanently – but it hasn't . I have searched grain industry literature and news articles but cannot find any mention of such a discovery. The market must be in error, an aberration. I have stumbled on it by accident. No-one else has realised it yet. Prices must correct before long and then we will profit.'

'Are you saying I can't lose?' I said.

'It is an ideal investment,' said Wilbur. 'A spread controls against internal risks like the weather and protects against external risks, like innovation.'

'Excellent. I'll be in it.'

Wilbur introduced me to his broker and I transferred $6000, $3000 of it for wheat at 380 dollars per tonne and $3000 for a short on barley at 275 dollars per tonne.

That afternoon the broker left a message for me to call him.

'Margin call,' he said. 'Your wheat is down to $370 per tonne but barley has gone up, to $280 per tonne. What are you going to do?'

I bit my lip.

'Holy shit. This wasn't supposed to happen. Wheat was supposed to go up and barley was supposed to go down, widening the gap. But the opposite is happening. What's going on?'

'Nothing new,' he said. 'Just normal trading.'

'I hope Wilbur knows what he is doing,' I thought.

'How much have I lost?' I asked.

'You are down $10/tonne on wheat and you will have to pay $5 more per tonne on your barley short.

'How much altogether?'

'You have 3000 tonnes of wheat, so that loss is $30,000. You will have to pay an additional $5 per tonne for 3000 tonnes of barley, or $15,000. All together you are down $45,000 and your deposit of $6,000 won't cover it. Deposits on spreads are at a margin of 5%, amounting to 20 times your deposit of $6,000 = $120,000. Your deposit is enough at present.

'I'll hold position and hope the trend turns around,' I said. I did not feel at all comfortable with so much money at stake.

The following morning the broker phoned again.

'Margin call. The gap has continued to narrow,' he said. 'Your deposit is gone. Will you put in another $6000?'

'Barley is going up faster than wheat is coming down. The gap is narrowing. I can't afford to hold both.'

'Then break a leg.'

'Which one?'

'I'll keep the wheat, hoping it will begin going up.'

'And the barley?'

'I'll close it. It's up $5 per tonne for 3000 tonnes, or $15,000.'

'You'll have to pay the full cost of the barley, $825,000 as it will be outside a spread and not on margin,' said Wilbur. 'I would hate to be exposed like you, with a short of $825,000 on barley. If you keep it, at settlement date, if there has been a shortage of barley, a weather event, or demand from the malthouses, come September you might not be able to buy it for love or money. Then you could lose your shirt. You would be wise to take your loss now.'

'I'll take my loss of $15,000 on the barley with my deposit of $6,000. I'll write you a cheque for $9,000. I wasn't expecting this and it hurts.'

I closed the barley future and transferred $9,000 to the broker to cover my loss.

'You still have the wheat and if you don't find a buyer, in September you will have to take delivery,' he said. 'If there has been a glut, you could receive several railway wagons filled with wheat that no-one wants, paying transport and storage, losing most of the $3000 you paid. I wouldn't be able to sleep at night. You had better pray the price starts going up, due to bad weather, crop failure or wheat disease, in America, China or Russia.'

'Why did you expose me to this?'
'My prediction said you couldn't lose.'
'Your prediction was shit.'
'My prediction was okay,' said Wilbur. 'Shit happens.'

For the next three weeks, I anxiously studied world weather reports and wheat price trends. I was relieved when the September wheat price increased. A week before the end of term I sold it at a profit of $10,000. With my loss of $15,000 on the barley, my overall loss was $5,000. I would have to borrow it somehow. My father would notice the trading in his account. He never gambled himself and would not like my profligacy.

I was desperate.

I asked Wilbur 'Would you lend me $5,000 until the end of the year?'

'I would like to, but I am in a hole too,' Wilbur said. 'I am hanging on to get the quitters' money.'

'My money!'

'To profit you have to stay in the game. Your wheat could come good.'

My barley short had taken up more than my initial deposit and was closed. My long on wheat had held its own for several days now.

'It might recover,' I said hopefully.

'It's a risky business,' said Wilbur. 'That's why my money is all tied up. Sorry Tom.'

'That's okay. I'll get a loan from someone else.'

There were a couple of people I could try before I sold my car.

'The theory is sound,' I thought. *'Too bad the commodities didn't do what they were supposed to. The prices went against the odds. If the deal was in girls, there would be a good chance of coming out ahead.'*

In a love straddle, I would be transacting the commodity love, not as a subjugator of women but as a speculator. Women and men would consent to be matched, with their consent. They would benefit from opportunities to enter a love match by participation in a larger market. Love is necessarily tenuous and temporary but within a love market, exchange could be more secure. By commodifying love, the vagaries of love trading, such as fraud and bigamy, could be greatly reduced or even eliminated. I would try it, pioneering selling Vicki short in a love trade.

CHAPTER 24 VULNERABLE

'Could you lend me $5000 until the end of the week?' I asked Larry.
'Shit. What have you done?'
I told him about the grains straddle and unexpected result.
'Archer, you are a bloody fool!'
'It seemed quite safe.'
'So did the South Sea Company. I can only lend you $500. Lisa and I are getting married and we need every bean.'
'Thanks — five hundred would help. I'll try the others first. I may take you up on it.'
'Ask Richard. He's rolling in it.'
Richard was in the kitchen making a bacon butty.
'Richard, I need to borrow $5000 by the end of the week.'
'Have you tried everyone else?'
'I have borrowed against my father's overdraft account, but I need to repay it urgently.'
'Let's get this right,' Richard said. 'You have grabbed a piece of your old man's credit and now you want me to save your ass by giving you some of mine. Am I a sucker, or what?'
'It isn't exactly like that. I had some bad luck. Shit happens.'
'Let me think about it. Ask me tomorrow.'
The next day Richard came into my room where I was studying.
'Tom, I can get the money for you, but there is a condition.'
'What?'
'You would have to stop chasing Vicki. I want her.'
I was surprised but pleased. I might have suggested it in return for a loan. I knew Richard wanted her but I didn't think he stood a chance. She hadn't shown much interest in him so far. I had nothing to lose and money to gain by conceding his suitor position, which

was virtually defunct. Was it possible Richard's prospects with Vicki were as good as he imagined?

CHAPTER 25 GIRLS SPREAD

I found Wilbur in the coffee bar and told him that Richard might pay to get access to Vicki.

'I have seen how grains are bought and sold as commodities. People use the market to supply them with what they need and to make a profit when they have something to sell,' I said. 'Could people who want a partner, or who want to finish with a partner, search in a love market? There could be a trading floor, or an online display, or an app, offering exchanges.'

'It satirises love matching,' said Wilbur. 'Love is monetized, demeaning and ridicules the romantic element. It's too dangerous. I'd stick to grains. Love between a man and a woman is supposed to be a unique match, not like a miller with a recipe to purchase a future trainload of grain.'

'But love is a trade, isn't it?'

'Yes, of a type,' Wilbur said. 'Males and females exchange their values.'

'Do they balance?'

'It is difficult to calculate, but balancing is an ideal, yes.'

'Why?'

'If one side does most of the taking, the giver could resent it,' said Wilbur.

'Because the other is taking unfairly?'

'Yes. However, a fair exchange in love is not always possible.'

'Coupledom does have agreement though,' said Tom.

They looked around at other students in the bar, mostly couples intent on each other.

'Couples negotiate relationships: that is their main intercourse,' Tom said.

'A love match would exchange more than material value,' said Wilbur. 'The couple would agree to devote their interests, skills and wealth to each other.'

'Like with a dowry?'

'Wider than that. A bride can supply a dowry as part of the price a man is demanding for his commitment,' said Wilbur. 'He would get her loyalty, income, possessions, beauty, personality and her 'chemistry'. She could have many features he would value. Different men would rate wants variously, depending on the woman.'

'Not to mention access to her reproductive organs and maternal caring,' I said.

'The matters for negotiation could be extensive,' said Wilbur.

'Her wants would differ from a man's,' I said.

'What do you suppose a woman would want from a man?' Wilbur asked.

'Access to his affection, physique, character, income, prospects, material assets, sperm and money,' said Tom. 'There could be many things. Ideally contributions of the woman and the man would balance.'

'That seems unlikely.'

'They can fine tune by negotiating what they will exchange.'

'Including certain rights to each other.'

'No woman will consent to give up her rights to a man,' said Wilbur, shocked. 'A man can't own a woman.'

'No, she can't be repossessed like a chattel. The trade is not about rights of possession but what each will voluntarily bring to a mutually respectful union.'

CHAPTER 26 LOVE MATCH

'A love match is more than an economic transaction. Love is for keeps,' I said.

'Finding a partner with the skills you want seems straightforward,' said Wilbur.

'Economics is only one of several possible dimensions of the exchange,' I said. 'They can have as much emotion and psychological involvement as they want. It is up to them how economic and material they get. Negotiations can take several years.'

'Sometimes love is everything,' said Wilbur. 'Couples commit to love each other and haggle later about things they will share.'

'It's not usual to talk about money and possessions, is it?' I asked.

'Negotiating material considerations before the wedding could be unacceptable in some social circles,' Wilbur said. 'It could seem to revive historical practices that overrode a woman's right to self-determination.'

'There is no fear of that,' I said. 'This is progressive: she can choose a partner or stay single. There would be a legal contract, not unlike a prenuptial agreement.'

'Prenups are about reserving assets, not about trading them,' said Wilbur.

'Isn't a pre-nup a trade? It reserves the minimum price each would pay.'

'Not really,' Wilbur said. 'A prenup agreement is about what is yours, what is hers and what each of you will take away if you separate.'

'Same thing,' I said. 'If a man pulled out and took back his interest in a female, wouldn't that be like selling her?'

'If she consented.'

'What if he wasn't in a relationship with her — could he sell her short?' asked Tom.

'Of course, supposing he could find a buyer who she will consent to accept,' Wilbur said doubtfully. 'He would have to get her back, or get another girl like her, to deliver on settlement day.'

CHAPTER 27 CONSENT

In a class-free interval, he had coffee with Steve. He told him about his agreement with Richard. Steve was astonished.
 'Selling your girlfriend is a joke, isn't it?'
 'No. I'm serious. I will sell Vicki to Richard for $5000 for delivery before July 31st.'
 'But you don't possess Vicki.'
 'I will by then, even if I have to pay more for her.'
 'Vicki can't be sold and bought like a thing.'
 'I agree. She can refuse.'
 'Refuse what?'
 'To partner the buyer.'
 'Why would she give her consent?'
 'She could want to be with me. It's entirely voluntary.'
 'It foregrounds money, when it should be offstage.'
 'Financing of the deal would be offstage, between Richard and me. This is not a misogynistic scheme to exploit a sex slave. She already knows him and can choose to accept him or not, on her own terms. In fact, she is more likely to get the guy she wants than if she leaves it to chance.'
 'Why do you want to sell her?'
 'I can't afford her and I need the money.'
 '$5000 compensates me for getting a hold on Vicki in the future and denying demands of other men who could want her.'
 '$5000 isn't much of a price for a woman like Vicki, when you think about her asset value. It's far less than the value of her earning potential, cost of her education and her property value. Richard is getting off lightly.'
 'I agree, but I couldn't ask him for more.'
 'Why not?'

'He has to go to his parents for the money. If she is too expensive, they might balk.'

'Could you get the money by selling Barbara?'

'I need her until after finals, when I will set her up with another engineering student. If I get a First, Barbara will get kudos. An ambitious man will value a woman who has been with someone successful like me.'

'You really are up yourself, aren't you? An ex-Tom girl would in fact be stigmatised.'

'On the contrary, she would have had a successful relationship and be able to use her experience to attract another partner. If a man wants her, but lacks the means, I could forego my brokerage.'

'It's a scam! You are a rake!'

'How so?'

'A rake speculates in casual love. He commits to a girl and when he has made a profit, he reneges on the deal. A rake never intends to transfer his assets, but she cannot detect the difference between his offer and that of a genuine buyer. His honour is in tatters and she loses social standing.'

'You are trying to get Vicki by delaying your move on her until you have finished your studies and have a job lined up. You are trying to keep Richard away from her by getting him to pay for exclusive access to her and encouraging him to make his pitch early. It is a scam.

'Relationships often don't have total commitment at the start. Barbara can leave me, or Richard, or anyone, whenever she wants.'

'She might think she can reform you.'

'It is not necessary.'

'No other woman would ever want to go near you again.'

'Don't be so sure. Women like independent men. They don't want a spaniel. I will be able to command a high price.'

'You may be intelligent, but you are socially obnoxious and your ideas about how to bond with girls are crap,' said Steve.

'I haven't noticed you dripping with blondes. Vicki is at the top of the girls' ladder because she is popular with guys. She can command a very high price in commitments, obligations and conditions. For a guy she wants, she can lower her price.'

'For someone as weird as you, her price would be 'Not For Sale',' Steve said.

'What do you mean 'weird'?'

'You don't seem to have emotions, Tom. A guy and a gal commit to each other a bit at a time, so they can pull out without losing face, without being relegated down their gender hierarchies. A girl doesn't wear a price tag visible to all-comers, or reveal any price at all.'

'The prices are hidden from view,' Tom said. 'Vicki's 'price' sums up her conditions for entering into an exclusive relationship. Her demands now are more than I can provide. But when I have graduated and am in a good job, her price could be within reach.'

'Tom, you are playing with bloody fire!' Steve said. 'You are trying to resolve issues of love, loyalty and morality by an economic strategy.'

'Correct. She is a bad buy at her current price. I can get her for less later.'

'If you get lucky,' said Steve.

'Love is risky. You have to put yourself out there.'

'Rather you than me.'

'Where's your sense of adventure? This could be fun,' I said. 'Try it yourself with Angela and Margot.'

Stephen shook his head. 'It's all a prank to you, isn't it? Women will despise you. Some men will too.'

I sensed that Steve was envious of the deal I had created. He didn't have a deal with a girl.

CHAPTER 28 COMMODIFYING LOVE

Steve's arguments about the emotionality of love dismayed me. I loved women and wanted to benefit them. Commodifying love would bring transparency to relationships that could be flawed. Those who would object most would be unable to negotiate a match, because they were impecunious or pretending to have assets. A love market would thwart inequitable relationships and would be just.

My method offered men a way to secure a partner in the future when they could not secure a relationship now. They would receive from another suitor a payment to stand aside until a time when they can make their best offer. A templated contract agreement like mine could prompt them to form a liaison with a girl of their dreams.

Nor was a spread unjust when it allowed substitution of partners.

'It is not different to what happens when a lover has a bit on the side,' I said, 'except that instead of the two relationships being concurrent, they would be serial and more respectable.'

'You are bucking tradition,' said Steve. 'It's like with any social innovation; people won't understand it at first.'

'There is nothing illegal.'

'They will imagine this scheme could expose them to new dangers and not want a bar of it. The law may not be enough to protect them.'

'How can they be suspicious of a scheme that requires mutual consent?' I said. 'It has none of the compulsion of a 'shot-gun wedding.'

'Women will oppose you.'

'When they see it working, they'll welcome it.'

'Are you going to short sell Vicki?'

'Yes. I can't afford her now. I may be able to after exams. She will be free to choose between Richard or me, or someone else, or no-one at all. I am creating opportunities for her. Commodification will emancipate her.'

'You are a cold-hearted, selfish and cynical bastard,' said Steve. 'You will deserve it if both women tell you to go to hell! How will you explain this to Vicki?'

'I won't. She hasn't been taking much interest in me lately.'

'On settlement day she will discover you sold her out and there will be hell to pay.'

'I will help Richard to make his pitch and cover any extra costs he has,' I said. 'If Vicki won't consent, I'll pitch to her. She doesn't need to know my deal with Richard fell through.'

'If she did, she would feel manipulated.'

'She won't know,' I said. 'Few people are privy to how their partner has chosen them. They may never know who else was in the running.'

'You are breaking too many rules, Tom,' said Steve. 'Commodifying Vicki will expose her to more suitors she does not want, conceal her individuality and prevent her finding a partner of her own choice. Her relationships will be monetized, reducing her choices.'

'I have to stop Vicki disrupting my work. She has upset me several times. By commodifying her I can deal with her at arm's length and get on with my study. I know it is a long shot, but it could work. It won't do any harm and it will pay off my debt.'

Later, Steve put his head into Tom's room and quoted Shakespeare's Julius Caesar:

'Yond Cassius has a lean and hungry look;
He thinks too much; such men are dangerous.'

'Nothing ventured, nothing gained,' I replied, smiling wryly.

'It will be a miracle if you bring it off,' Steve said. 'What a hoot!'

CHAPTER 29 DELIVERY CONTRACT

Later I met Richard to play tennis at the uni. I showed Richard the agreement I proposed.
'This is our agreement about Vicki,' I said. 'Would you sign it, please.'
Richard read it carefully.
Agreement

'I Tom Archer (The Seller) agree to sell short a love relationship with Vicki Hillstone (The Commodity) to Richard Armitage (The Buyer) with delivery at Flat 6, Byron Estate, Ennerton, Liverpool by July 31st, 1967 (Settlement Day) with her consent. The Buyer agrees to pay The Seller 5000 dollars on the condition that The Seller avoids all amorous contact with The Commodity before Settlement Day. If, lacking her consent, The Commodity is not delivered to the Buyer, nor an acceptable substitute provided, the Seller's obligation under this contract will have been fulfilled.

Signed Seller:

_____

Tom Archer

Signed Buyer:

_____

Richard Armitage

Agreement Date: November 16th 1966
STRICTLY CONFIDENTIAL

Richard finished reading. 'Why does it have to be in writing?'

'We would forget.'

'It's not that fucking serious.'

'It fucking is,' I said. 'I am concerned that Vicki could find out about it and misunderstand. If you blab I will tell her you paid me 5000 bucks for her.'

'It was your idea,' said Richard.

I said to him: 'Okay, here's the deal you agreed to.

'If you sign this, You will pay me $5000 and I will be honour bound to stay away from Vicki until July 31st. She can go to you when she wants. If she doesn't go to you, then she can go to me if she wants.

'After July 31st.'

'That's right. Imagine that I have sold you Vicki for delivery by July 31st. I may be able to come up with another girl graduate for you. I am trying to sell Barbara as a girl secretary, if you're interested.

'Vicki could choose you, me or another man, or no-one at all. She could self-own without any male interest in her — a position a liberated girl like Vicki could prefer.'

'It's risky but it seems okay,' said Richard. 'What I hear you saying is you won't make any moves on her before July 31st.'

'What is Vicki supposed to do?'

'She can do whatever she wants.'

'What will you be doing with Barbara, Tom? Do you have a deal with her?'

'Not as a part of our deal. I could place her with some well-off engineering student who wants a girlfriend who has shown she is able to partner a hard-working engineering student.'

Richard laughed.

'Would Barbara agree to that?'

'Necessity is the mother of consent.'

'You bastard.'

'So we have a deal?' I asked.

He hesitated.

'Okay,' said Richard. 'I'll get your money.'

'Neither of us will look real good. I won't say anything.'
'No. Nor will I.'
'Do you have the cash?'
He handed it over. I counted the money.
'Sign.'
Richard signed. Tom handed him a copy of the contract and a receipt.

'It's all good,' he told himself. *'My relationship with Vicki will be at arms length until July, when I will buy her, or a substitute, for delivery to Richard, with her consent.'*

He thought of the song: 'I wanna hold your hand' and sang quietly: *'I'll get you in the end.'*

They began their tennis match. They were evenly matched. The games were fiercely fought, a contest of wills.

'30: 40,' said Tom as he bounced the ball before serving. 'You haven't got what it takes to win this game — or Vicki.'

'I'm doing better than you are,' said Richard.

'We'll see.'

Tom served, they rallied and he won the point.

'Deuce,' Tom said. 'Even with me out of the running, you still look bad. You won't have an advantage for long.'

'I'm saving your bacon, Archer. You should be grateful.'

They played the point.

'Advantage server.'

'Vicki is fortunate that you will be off her case,' said Richard. 'A girl shouldn't have to put up with a control freak like you.'

'Fuck you Armitage. At least I have gone after her fairly, without having to pay off the competition.'

Tom served and won.

'Game.'

The signing of the contract meant Tom would no longer be distracted by Vicki's antics. It was a relief. He could forget about her, until at the end of the year when he had a degree and a job. There would be fewer students around, demand for her would be reduced and her price would be lower. He might be able to afford her.

To implement the straddle while expressing interest in getting together with her later, he would withdraw from her. It was a tricky message and he wanted to deliver it personally. He tried to meet with her but she rudely put him off. He would not try again. She could infer that she was on his back burner.

'Maybe she'll be more tender if she simmers for a while,' he thought.

PART 3: ACCEPTING

I had tried very hard to make Vicki my girl friend. I had pursued my desire for her first observing traditional matching protocols at the university, pushed aside social class differences, used dating psychology and finally employed commodity economics. But none of these had succeeded in attracting Vicki and she had turned away.

My plan was to be with Vicki after July 31st but as the date approached she showed no interest. As I prepared to leave England, to commence a job in Canada, I prepared to farewell my family and friends.

CHAPTER 30 FLING

One Saturday morning, Roger gave me a message that Vicki was having a party at her place that evening and I was invited.

'*Why didn't she ask me herself?*' I thought.

Because I had an agreement with Richard not to chase Vicki, I did not reply to the invitation and went on a date with Barbara.

On the following morning, I was studying at home when Roger dropped in.

'Hey, Tom, Richard screwed Vicki last night,' he said. 'He spent the night with her after the party.'

'Whaaat?' I could hardly believe it. Richard had taken delivery of Vicki months earlier than I expected, indeed I hadn't expected it to happen at all, though there was nothing written in the contract to prevent it. It was an oversight.

'I thought she was your girl?' said Roger.

It was an epithet that was music to my ears. I hadn't heard this lately and wondered if Roger was trying to cause trouble.

'Not anymore,' I said ruefully. 'This is the end.'

I had to sit down. Room and furniture rocked as my heart pumped adrenalin for a fight with Richard. He had gone behind my back. I tried to think what it meant for my relationship with Vicki. It could be over. A heavy curtain of grief descended.

'*I sold my rights in Vicki to him,*' I thought. '*We agreed he would wait until after July 31st.*'

Realistically, I couldn't expect to have my short cake and eat it, but I had never expected her to accept Richard. I had imagined he would try to get together with her after Finals.

With her rejection, my evaluation of myself plummeted.

'*I won't get her now,*' I thought gloomily. '*Vicki, why did you do this to me?*'

My chagrin primed me to hit back. When Richard came in, I confronted him.

'Did you fuck Vicki last night?'

Richard sighed, nodding gravely, looking away. 'Yeh.'

'Was she a virgin?'

He shook his head. 'No. There was a guy in Spain, when she was with her family on holiday.'

My intuition was that Richard was telling the truth. I wondered if I should fight him. I did not see that a punch-up would achieve anything, even if I won.

Richard didn't apologize. I had renounced my claim to Vicki when I sold her to him and took up with Barbara. But the code of honour that one should respect a mate's relationship still applied. Richard's going with Vicki was bad form.

I recalled Oscar Wilde's words: *'A good friend will always stab you in the front.'*

'Why do you think she did it?' I asked Steve despondently when he dropped in.

'You told me you had cut her adrift,' he said. 'She was free to find another guy. What did you expect? Didn't you have a deal with Richard about her?'

'Richard wasn't supposed to get her until after July 31st. The bastard broke our rules.'

'Why would he do that?'

'She probably put him up to it. Going with a flat mate's girl without asking is hostile. Perhaps she got wind of our deal and wanted a fling with Richard to drive a wedge between me and Richard, destroying our friendship.'

'Maybe you had hurt her. Did she know why you dropped her?'

'I was going to tell her but she was so avoiding me, I didn't get to talk to her…'

'Well, you botched it,' Steve said. 'I warned you.'

'Richard ratted on me. Going with a mate's girl is a foul.'

'Did Richard know you still wanted Vicki?'

'I agreed to stay away from her until the end of July, when he could try for her.'

'So why shouldn't he try for her before?' Steve asked.

'We had a verbal agreement. Not everything was written down.'
'Richard wouldn't want to wait. What about Vicki?'
'She didn't know about our agreement. If she had she wouldn't like us manipulating her.'
'That's true. What will you do now?'
'I'll try to forget. I'll keep on studying as if nothing has happened. What else can I do?'
'You could forgive them.'
'I can't ignore how they have dissed me.'
'Richard's agreement to stay away from her wasn't written down. Vicki would hardly respect you if she knew you had sold her.'
'She might have gone with Richard to demonstrate she could do what she liked.'
'That's most likely,' I said. 'Why would Vicki want me, when I have delayed our relationship and been beaten to the scoring line by Richard?'

CHAPTER 31 RETALIATION

When Richard and Vicki didn't stay together, I expected Richard to ask me to return the $5,000 he had paid for access to her until the end of the course, July 31st. Now he had taken delivery early, I was under no obligation to return his money and I could take up with her earlier, if she wanted. But Vicki showed no interest in me. Her tryst with Richard had intruded into my prospects with her and couldn't be ignored. But what to do?

I still had a spread, with a short on Vicki and a long on Barbara. I could profit from the narrowing gap of the spread, if Vicki's price was increasing and Barbara's decreasing. But the fling was evidence that the gap was widening and I was losing. Fortunately I had not been able to place the spread, because my love commodity was experimental, so I didn't lose any money.

Thinking I had been outmanoeuvred, I beat myself up. When Vicki and Richard's tryst did not develop into a relationship, her rejection and Richard's disrespect rankled and my hurt eased a little. My short had been closed. My interest in Vicki was ended, unless I made a new bid for her, but it was unlikely to succeed. I grieved for what I had lost, like death of a friend.

'Was she merely inconsiderate or did she deliberate her malice towards me?'

I was not going to take it lying down. My urge to punch Richard subsided and I focussed on exacting revenge less dramatically, by withdrawing from helping him with our studies. Richard was going for a First Class degree too.

The work had stepped up to a higher level of difficulty.

'What did you get for the assignment?' Richard asked me.

'A.'

'I got B. I thought we had the same solution. Did you go on and do more work?'

'I can't remember.'

'Can I have a look?' asked Richard.

'No. Get fucked.'

I wanted no part in normalising his achievement.

Slowly and inexorably I pursued my revenge. I was one of the leaders whose work was passed around and copied, but now I kept my answers to myself and handed them in without showing Richard, who struggled to keep up.

After Easter, the class rounded the home turn with only Finals ahead. Our studies required long hours of hard work. I was fortunate to have Barbara to relax me. When I picked her up for our weekly date, my head would be spinning with formulae, unable to do small talk. Gradually, she brought me back to earth and restored me for the gruelling week ahead.

My feelings for Vicki were ambivalent. She had shot herself in the foot, disqualifying herself from my attention. I wondered what I had done to deserve her cavalier and hurtful rejection. Her fling with Richard had spurned my feelings. Her motives were puzzling. I had regarded her as a gazelle, a dainty shy herbivore, but now she seemed more like a secretive, sleek and dangerous feline who had mauled me badly. Despite my wounds, I still wanted her. If she would apologise, our friendship could recover.

I took Barbara on dates to country pubs. She drank Babycham and we ate wholesome inn fare. We strolled along country lanes in the local hills and then sped back to my bed. She had me drive her home in the middle of the night to sneak into her parents' home like a teenager, as if what we had been doing was illicit. Our relationship was convenient. It brought me emotional security and the stability I needed to devote myself to study.

Initially I harboured ill feelings for both Richard and Vicki. It was too late to undo their actions but I got satisfaction from cutting off contact with them. This inconvenienced Richard, but there was nothing with Vicki that I could withdraw from. I had not achieved any part of the outcome I had wanted. I was not proud of my retaliation against Richard and I realized that I had botched my short sale of Vicki rather than being a victim of Richard's greed.

The outcome was that I was nowhere with Vicki, despite all my efforts to present myself acceptably at the appropriate time. Vicky continued to be cold and distant with me. The tension between Richard and me weakened and as the end of my course neared the incident diminished in significance and Vicki was just another student experimenting with relationships.

CHAPTER 32 LIVESTOCK JUDGING

The outcome removed Vicki from my consideration at the culmination of my university studies when I had accepted a job offer in Canada. I had hoped that Vicki would want to be with me as I prospered in my job.

I hadn't allowed that Vicki was pursuing a career of her own, with a job in the UK. Men had been used to having women follow them abroad, often with inferior job prospects.

Selecting a partner for life benefited from my experience of growing up managing livestock: the ability to evaluate health, breeding potential and value after butchering for sale to the public. The consumption viewpoint was not applicable to selecting a partner, but it included understanding of human anatomy, biomechanics and internal processes.

English Young Farmers' Clubs ran stock judging competitions in which contestants had to place four animals, A, B,C and D, in order of worth for breeding, or for meat, or milk, stating reasons to a panel of seasoned breeders. The challenge was to imagine the animals calving and producing milk, or hung in a butcher's cold room. The characteristics that counted included skeletal conformance, feeding efficiency, mating and birthing ability. I was rather good at making correct inferences and delivered succinct appraisals persuasively to panels of judges. I learned from my father how to make in depth comparisons of animals quickly and accurately. Our Club entered me in the Bridgwater show to compete with able young farmers from throughout the district. The skills of evaluating physiques and temperaments were useful for selecting girlfriends.

From a distance now, I wondered what were Vicki's qualities that had so obsessed me. I had admired her in the same way I judged livestock on the farm for their breeding points, utility and condition.

She was a splendid animal, capable of mothering wonderful offspring. She took great care with her health, although her physical fitness was probably lax as, her only sport was skiing. I had the same deficiency.

It wasn't obvious how we could be an English couple. Our interests didn't correspond. My training was engineering and Vicki's was psychotherapy. I regretted not trying to synthesize a joint approach earlier.

CHAPTER 33 WEATHER

The environment of our farm was being exploited for a nuclear power station and wind turbines. Local weather became the subject of intense interest.

Lord St Audries was an elderly man who owned many farms in Somerset. He lived modestly in a huge Elizabethan country house with one housekeeper. The first manor house was built as early as 1186 and occupied by the Acland Hood family for 8 centuries. It was largely rebuilt in Elizabethan times with a maze and large pleasure gardens.

The 2nd Baron St. Audries was born in 1893 and died in 1971 at age 77. He was educated at Eton and graduated from Oxford University, with a Master of Arts degree. He fought in the First World War between 1914 and 1919, gaining the rank of Lieutenant in the Somerset Light Infantry.

Our landlord was a wealthy aristocrat who had a penchant for careful observation of the weather. His hobby was unusual even in the UK, where weather recording is a respectable obsession.

He measured and recorded local weather, keeping temperature records, analysing for trends, highs and lows. He corresponded with weather enthusiasts and exchanged observations with weather enthusiasts in Sweden and Russia.

His analysis was Cartesian, omitting inferences and circumstantial evidence. It was often devoid of human values, without meaning of existence, beyond physical and biological processes. He lacked statistical understanding of the weather's effects on populations.

He took a kindly interest in his tenants, such as my family and he preserved the estate and country house and local traditions. I don't know if his interest in the weather passed to his successor, Lady

Gass, or to any other member of his family. Weather recording has become full-time work at weather stations equipped with automatic sampling systems.

Lord St Audries had investigated weather long before governments and universities were interested and the thrust of weather research was to measure the preservation and resilience of natural phenomena, before ecological effects of human technologies had been identified. For example, Rachel Carson in Silent Spring (1951) attributed deaths of hawks to the chemical pesticide DDT. Since then it has been revealed that her data was not sufficient to draw this conclusion and use of DDT for mosquito control has now resumed in some countries. Carson and aristocrats like Lord St Audries were in the vanguard of the environmental movement, which eventually embraced the Heidegger method and widened to include climate change.

Phenomena of the climate and weather have long been observed, especially by farmers who depend on them for success of their crops and livestock.

Heidegger (1889-1976) proposed that the subjective experience of an observer could affect the record he kept of the weather. Heidegger referred to the mode of being that he believed is particular to human beings as 'dasein' or 'existence.' He defined phenomenology as an approach to qualitative inquiry that aims to reflect on human experience by describing and interpreting experiential meanings as they are lived through, shaped by consciousness, language, and cultural understandings.

His thinking involved questioning and putting ourselves in question as much as the cherished opinions and doctrines we have inherited through our education, or our shared knowledge. His analysis questioned the potential of situations and set aside previous experience. He described humans' individual existences as being 'thrown' into the world.

'Your destiny can't be changed but, it can be challenged,' Heidegger said.

Analysis of trends in weather observations require carefully controlled and reported weather conditions that would defy the precision of Cartesian methods. Heidegger would regard the weather as a phenomenon, with its 'dasein' revealing potential, meaning 'existence' or 'being there'.

The section below is taken from my book Time Is Gold, Chapter 30, Phenomenology.

'The measurements assumed what was going on in people's heads, without being able to make measurements. Because they lacked objectivity, the analyses were 'subjective' and consequently down-rated.

'There was an attempt to observe behaviour reproducibly: to be objective; to control observation; to hide observers; to isolate subjects; to hypothesize; to falsify; to do tests with observers blinded and double-blinded.'

The method seems familiar because now it is widely used. His Lordship would have found the breadth of observations in weather recording nowadays astounding. His reflex would be to refer his science to Renee Descartes, who had the creed 'Cogito ergo sum', meaning 'I know I am because I think'. That was the belief of observers of human mating rituals, the ladder method of pairing and the effects on them of social class identity. More eclectic ideas have emerged. Lord St Audries' scrutiny of prospective marriage partners was possibly inhibited by his too thoughtful Cartesian gaze and by his great wealth. Perhaps that was the reason he never married.

My transition from Cartesian objectivity to Heideggerian phenomenology was gradual as I sought practical outcomes with Barbara and another girl, Chris. With her, I bundled, sharing a bed with our clothes on. The outcome was firmly in mind, which it wasn't with Barbara and my postmodern exploration by Heidegger's method.

CHAPTER 34 JANETTA

I learned to sail in the South Atlantic. The yacht Eshowe was a heavy steel vessel. She was ketch rigged but had few sailing alternatives and the crew had little to do because she was slow and did not speed up with adjustment of the sails. She was ponderous, like a digital model.

My next boat was Janetta, a sleek teak-on-oak sloop, harboured at Conyer Creek inside the Isle of Sheppey, on the River Thames below London. It was several years later and in the interim I had married Rita, with our first baby on the way. Janetta was a light sloop with a canoe stern, sensitive to the sails and rudder. She was like an analogue model and fun to sail. She slipped through the water and rode waves with aplomb. She kept me busy with the sails and helm.

In my first job I had been an engineer developing digital models from simpler analogue models. With the digital models, the method was to adjust the constants one by one until you obtained the result wanted. Analogue models allowed you to set groups of constants, all together, learning to get closer and closer to the wanted result.

Janetta was an analogue sailing craft, more enjoyable to sail than the larger and heavier South African vessel Eshowe.

We had sailed for a couple of years in the Thames Estuary when we decided to go over to France. It was fine summer weather and after packing food and bedding we set off. We were carried up the Channel by the tide as far as Belgium and then back again by the same tide. When we reached the jetty at Calais we were swept across the harbour entrance and it began to be doubtful whether we would be able to get in. I scrambled to start the engine, a very old Norton Villiers without a muffler. It banged away and seemed certain to shake all the caulking out from between our hull planks. More by luck than design we got into the harbour and tied up at a quay. We spent a couple of days exploring Calais, eating excellent food at restaurants.

On the way back we had trouble. There was a sudden change in the wind direction which capsized us and we sat in a cockpit filled with water, about to sink. My wife, who had been admirably patient so far, was concerned about our foetus, as was I.

'Get me off this boat,' she said emphatically.

We limped back and beached at Ramsgate.

We went ashore leaving Janetta resting on her keel. Then the tide ran out leaving the boat balanced, ready to crash to one side any second. When it fell, this dislodged the caulking remaining after the shaking by the engine's vibrations.

When we tried to steer the leaking boat out and up the Thames, the rudder handle broke and the rudder dropped off. I rigged an oar to steer with and we eventually reached home port at Conyer Creek.

I learned not to take risks with an old boat, with a pregnant woman aboard, in unfamiliar waters. Our capsize was unfortunate. Janetta responded to sensitive handling but needed caulking and a new rudder. Sailing Janetta fulfilled my goals of skippering on the high seas and later I bought a bigger boat, in better shape. Varnishing her teak deck and sailing her was timeout from my life, an analogue experience.

CHAPTER 35 FLYING

Learning to pilot light planes in Canada was another algorithmic experience of adjusting conditions for flight to make the aircraft go where I wanted. I had trained in ground school and logged the required hours with an instructor, eventually flying solo. Learning to fly had an algorithmic procedure for monitoring the various systems. Compared with sailing, it was automatic and unforgiving, with more dire consequences. This was not what I wanted from flying. How I envied the glider pilots I met who after being towed aloft, flew freely from thermal to thermal across the Australian continent.

Soon after receiving a pilots' licence, I spent several days flying practice circuits at Edmonton airport, together with about a dozen planes doing the same thing. I wanted to show off my aerial competence to Rita and invited her to accompany me on a short flight the next day.

'Sorry, but I'm busy with visitors all day tomorrow,' she said. 'I could come the day after.'

It was agreed. I would fly by myself tomorrow. I needed the practice, as I wanted things to go perfectly when I took Rita up. She would be my first passenger and I wanted to impress her.

After taking off, the intercom informed me that I should switch to a runway at right angles because the wind had changed direction. The planes in the circuit changed from the new take-off, to a new crosswind leg, then downwind around a base leg and then a final approach to the landing. Most of the landings were 'touch and go' by pilots in training.

I followed the others around, at a distance of 1000 feet for commercial aircraft but less for light planes. When I reached the final approach, I lined up with the runway, lowered the flaps and landing gear, adjusting my air speed to descend to the runway apron where I would touch down.

When I landed I continued along the runway looking for a taxiway to reach the flying school plane park, but couldn't recall whether I should turn off left or right. I was still moving at about 100 kilometres per hour and before I had decided which way to go, we had reached and passed the taxiway junction. I continued along the main runway.

Then air traffic control screeched in my ear.

'Aircraft EAB 458, clear the runway.'

I continued, looking for the next taxiway to take.

'EAB 458 clear the runway immediately. There is a commercial aircraft on final.'

A few seconds later, there was the roar of a Boeing 707 jet passing low overhead and we bounced in the jet wash. He had aborted his landing and would have to fly 50 kilometres around to try again.

I found a taxiway and headed back. The control tower reamed me out for endangering other traffic. He was indignant and yelling.

I was shaken by his reprimand but was relieved that my incompetence had not caused an accident, nor had it occurred tomorrow when Rita would be with me.

I put Rita off until later, hoping I would gain confidence, but I never flew again. I had realised that my memory for direction was poor and that I didn't enjoy the procedural discipline needed to fly safely.

Heidegger described the danger of technology in displacing beings from what they originally were, hindering our ability to experience them truly. I didn't find flying relaxing. I felt displaced, lacking true experience.

Sailing in Australia's Moreton Bay suited me much better, for the land I encountered was sand banks at low speeds. It was a more forgiving environment, with less urgency to avoid collisions.

My training to fly was quite extensive but my near accident ended my interest. I got off lightly. I had an outcome of man and machine that ended well.

CHAPTER 36 VOLKSWAGEN

When I obtained my first car, my intention had been to drive it well, without fooling around or endangering others.

It was a lefthand drive Volkswagen beetle. Overtaking was difficult on 3-lane roads in the UK because oncoming vehicles weren't immediately visible when I began pulling out to overtake. Driving it was like playing Russian Roulette.

The engine was almost worn out and lacked power. I attached a vacuum cleaner hose to the top of the carburettor and ran the hose through the back of the car and onto the blower hose of the floor heater. Pressurised air was turbo-charged into the carburettor. I imagined it provided a large increase in power.

When it broke down, I was fortunate to receive a much better car from my parents. I proceeded to re-engineer the Volkswagen as a go-cart. I shortened the chassis and changed the controls for sitting astride the central transmission arch.

Heidegger's phenomenology had helped me look for unused potential that had been overlooked by the manufacturer.

A problem was that with most of the body removed, the front wheels bounced along the ground. The solution was to carry a passenger for ballast and my younger brother obliged.

We had a lot of fun speeding around the farm, sliding around corners as I practiced the agency that I explored as an engineer.

Sailing and flying had interested me in the phenomena of aerodynamics, until I could predict movement of the craft in rough conditions. Heidegger's attention to all the potential in flight or sailing always found points of interest or adjustments to test.

My Volkswagen go-cart fulfilled my interest in engineering a vehicle. It confirmed my interest in engineering. Thereafter, I adapted and maintained several cars.

CHAPTER 37 RITA

Whenever I caught up with Vicki and suggested getting together, she became interested in my children and Rita. At first I had thought she did not want to be a home wrecker. It was an interest that induced loyalty in me. Vicki kept me at arm's length, although it seemed she would have taken over the girls without compunction if asked.

Rita and I had no other interests keeping us together and when Sarah and Tegan left home, we separated. Rita minded her granddaughter Alexa when Tegan went away for work.

When Rita left me, I had thought I would never see her again. Now I would see her at Atrium Apartments and see photos of her with her daughters and mothering her grandchildren in the UK and Australia.

According to Claude Levi-Strauss (1908-2009), myths are a means of gaining insight into the human spirit because the unconscious, collective mythological imagination is relatively untouched by a community's other vital structures and by the social and economic dimensions. Myths (oral) come into being by a process of transformation of one myth into another.

The absence of communication between Rita and me left our myths raw and untended.

One outcome of my separation from Rita was my isolation. She had brought me to Australia and my social life in Australia had been with her family. Suddenly I found myself alone, surrounded by a wall of silence. When Tegan, Alexa, Sarah, Uly and Dorian visited me it was a good outcome.

CHAPTER 38 NEIGHBOURS

I had wanted Tegan and Alexa to live beside me as neighbours with whom I would have regular interaction, but I saw them infrequently. After Tegan and Alexa had settled into their apartment, their withdrawal from me was hurtful. I had imagined I could mind Alexa when her mother went out and I could observe Alexa's progress in her new school. But apart from a piece of pie now and then and going to watch Alexa play basketball, contact with them was less than weekly. Myths of natural family togetherness belied the social reality that we lived almost independently.

Levi Straus's theory was that social relations have a particular structure. The structure of a system determines the position of the whole. It also affects the position of each part of the whole. The problem was that we never agreed a family social structure and I didn't know what part, if any, was mine as grandfather.

Neighbourly interaction between us bumped along at an unprecedented low. This seemed quite normal to me, although I didn't like it. When I left home 60 years ago, I had not kept in close contact with my parents. I had written letters and gone home from Canada and Australia at five year intervals. It wasn't enough. Contact with my family in the UK had become stilted and brief. Contact with my siblings had virtually ceased. I suppose they thought I might return to the UK some day, but I received no invitation nor plans.

Tegan used Rita and an assortment of friends to take care of Amani, without informing me who would be there if there was any trouble and I could be involved.

Other incidents were Tegan's complaints about the state of my apartment.

'You need to wash the kitchen floor!'

Tegan had trained as a microbiologist and was obsessive about cleaning. I kept my place clean to my own standard but Tegan offered to have her cleaner do my place. I paid several times but when the complaining ended I wondered if that was the reason she seldom visited my place or there was another reason.

Tegan offered to order my groceries weekly on line, which she did reliably and conscientiously for months. I was very thankful, because carrying heavy groceries on the bus was difficult with my sore back.

Tegan was self-employed and had to work hard for her contracts to be renewed.

Tegan bought a share in a yacht and took Amani sailing frequently. I wanted to go too, but my balance was unreliable and I couldn't help on deck or at the jetty, so I stayed ashore and relived my memories of sailing.

Social outcomes have been beyond my control. I tried to broach the topic.

'I don't suppose I'll see you for the next week,' I said to Tegan.

'When do you want to see us?'

'More often than that. I had hoped we would share our lives better.'

'What do you want to do?'

'Talk about feelings and people. Share experiences.'

'How would we do that?'

'Talk about what we like and dislike.'

'For example?'

'How I feel alone sometimes. Worries that you have.'

'Would you expect us to visit and keep you company?'

'Yes I want to see more of you and other people while I still can.'

'But you don't like having visitors. You are an introvert. You would soon want to be alone.'

'No, I like having people over. Another reason is I want to sort out my things and accounts before I forget how. It would be good to discuss what I need to do.'

'It sounds like you want to make final arrangements. Wouldn't that be too depressing?'

'Not if I tackle it a bit at a time.'

'When do you want me to come?'
'When you have a couple of hours free one evening.'
'I'll let you know.'

CHAPTER 39 CHESS WITH SARAH

Sarah and her boys, Nico and Lucas, lived in England and it was difficult to keep in contact. If I set my alarm on a Wednesday night for 5am, Sarah would come online with a chessboard at 6 am, which was 9 pm in the UK. It should have been easy, but when the clocks changed in the UK it threw out our timing. Sometimes Sarah would cancel because she had too much going on with her boys. It wasn't often she cancelled. Chess games with Sarah were a mainstay of my weekly schedule.

Although Sarah was busy with her children and her job, she made time regularly to play. Sarah regularly thrashed me. She opened aggressively, placing her queen at my end of the board, supported by knights or bishops. Often it was checkmate in under 10 moves. The outcome could have been humiliation, but I didn't mind because she played so well. She was the only person who I would never mind losing to.

Sarah was a very good chess player and almost always beat me. We played mostly in silence, with only an occasional muttered expletive. I came away from these games bruised but thankful for Sarah's skill, which made for fast moving games.

After we had played a game, sometimes we would talk and Sarah would tell me how she was redecorating her house or her cottage at the coast. Our talk took in several topics of common interest, including her family, her job and her writing. We sometimes shared perceptions by means of myths, as suggested by Levi Strauss. Sarah had opinions about government and education, but she preferred going on strike rather than discussing politics. The intricacies of the British health, welfare and education systems seemed rife with myths and mystery. We talked sometimes about happenings in

England and I told her about developments in Australia that could interest her.

Although she had divorced, Sarah seemed content in England. Her former partner had custody of the boys for half of each week. Sarah could not bring them with her to Australia to live. Sadly I realised I would be fortunate to ever see them again. She had made a few close friends in Leicester and she sometimes met her English cousins or visited my sister Hazel in Bristol. She managed to keep her job at a time when universities were laying off staff. She put a lot of time into her job and I inferred she was successful.

My chess games with Sarah had a predictable social structure and it spread out to other interactions too. Our good communication was explained by Levi-Strauss' theory that sociality is maintained by a structure. The chess games had a definite structure.

PART 4: ADAPTED

I emigrated to Australia where there were only small cultural differences and I found it easy to adapt. After a decade employed in coal marketing, I became a science teacher concerned with the environment, energy resources and climate change. Australia had adaptated UK culture to local conditions. There were differences in thinking between the antipodes, but these were mainly in post-modern philosophies with differences behind the scenes and in media spectacles. A fresh perspective on Australian conditions emerged in my science teaching, with insights from the UK.

CHAPTER 40 STRANGER IN A STRANGE LAND

I had been in Australia for half of my life, but I often felt like a foreigner and I had difficulty conversing about important aspects of Australian life, such as drinking, sport and politics.

Although distribution of my inheritance had not brought me the close family living that I wanted, I heard from my daughters that they were making good use of my gift money. Tegan and Amani were enjoying living in their own apartment and Sharon had used her money to pay off the mortgage on her house in England and buy a small cottage by the coast in Norfolk. My gift was useful to Tegan for securing Amani's secondary schooling and for enabling Sharon to enjoy comfortable country living in a part of the UK she loved. I felt I had been able to make a real contribution to all of them.

I had lost interest in travelling either to Europe or around Australia. I was occupied taking care of myself, my home, my food, health and entertainment, communicating with family members when requested, or when necessary.

The common culture of England and Australia has a wealth of myths held in common, framing cultural structure as envisaged by Levi Strauss. I had so integrated in Australia that I now regarded myself as Australian, although there were a few matters where we were deeply divided, such as compulsory voting, preferential voting and climate change. Nothing I could say would persuade Australians to permit voluntary voting, because they treasured a history of enfranchisement shrouded in myths.

On most matters, I saw eye to eye with Australians. For my general well-being I preferred to investigate medical problems myself, in so far as I could. Through experience I had become suspicious of specialists who would subject me to dubious tests.

When I sought treatment for vertigo, dizziness, a GP prescribed Betahistine Dichloride. The pharmacist warned me: 'It can cause dizziness. Take one to three tablets per day as required.' I laughed. This side effect was the symptom to be treated. I preferred a self-treatment: Epley's Manoeuvre for Benign Positional Vertigo. This involved lying back quickly on a bed. It seemed unlikely, but it worked. It was peculiar, explained as movement of crystals in the head.

Health treatments may not be deterministic. My experience with vertigo and Epley's was not unlike how I replaced the battery in my watch. I searched Google 'To find how to change a battery in a Seiko watch.' A YouTube video explained how to remove the back of the watch and take out the battery. I bought a new one and followed the directions to fit it. I replaced the back but was disappointed when the hands were stationary. I asked Google 'How to start a Seiko watch after fitting a new battery?' The answer came back 'Drop it on the floor'. Overcoming scepticism, I did this and was surprised when the hands began moving.

I had seen small perturbations relieve blockages in other systems, such as flow of grain through a chute. Perhaps Epley's treatment had dislodged crystal grains needed for balance in my head.

I was sceptical of the efficacy of medical treatments. I had been taking two medications for a disorder for over thirty years, without knowing if they were benefitting me. I had no evidence that they were either harming or benefitting me. I tried to get help from a pharmacist.

'Can you sell me a placebo, similar in appearance to these medication pills, without the active ingredients?'

'No,' said the pharmacist. 'We do not sell placebos.'

'Can you make some?'

'Hmm. It's difficult. Ask your doctor. It may be possible.'

My doctor wasn't interested. I wondered if I purchased a mild analgesic medication, aspirin, in pills similar in appearance to the suspect medications, they could be tested as a placebo. Aspirin could thin blood, but I would be using only a small amount. I could alternate the pills daily for one of the medications, with the placebo, continuing for a week. The medication was for depression. When there was no change in my mood, I could continue for another week and replace the medication.

I loaded the pills into my prescription dispenser. The placebo pills were indistinguishable from my regular medications, avoiding any bias in writing up results.

Caution: Do not conduct a placebo test like this without first consulting a doctor.

I adapted my experience in the UK to Australian conditions. Often there was a synthesis of ideas. Medical doctors and pharmacists seemed to be as regulated by make believe and myths as are other aspects of Australian life. I was fortunate that I did not have a severe chronic condition. I refrained from seeking medical help unless I was seriously ill, exposing myself to doctors only when I really needed help.

Australia took some getting used to. Health professionals were quite unlike doctors in the British National Health Service. Their diagnoses were often transparent and precisely articulated, which was excellent, but the Australians had a similar system of payment for treatments and sometimes it was free 'bulk-billed' and at others expensive. I couldn't find anyone to explain how it worked. I cancelled my health insurance after 50 years having made very few claims.

CHAPTER 41 RABBITING

After church on Sundays in England, we would drive around the farm district looking over hedges at neighbours' farming, to see what they had been doing. I was pleased to get home and clean my rabbits' cages.

Albert's family caught most of their meat by rabbiting. A farm worker usually can't afford to buy beef or mutton from the butcher's. On Saturday mornings it was usual to see three generations of males in his family, walking along hedgerows of our farm carrying ferrets, terriers, nets, clubs and spades.

Their method was to go to a warren, peg the nets down over the bolt holes and put in the ferrets. After a minute or two, rabbits would explode into the nets and be despatched with clubs. Everyone knew what to do, orchestrated by Albert. The action ran fast and hot until the task became to recover the ferrets, which was difficult when they had made a kill underground and had to be dug out.

Rabbit meat was delicious. My mother would cook wild rabbits but refused the white rabbits I raised for their meat starting with a pair given me by a cousin. My purpose was to make a profit. Perhaps my mother was of the view that 'Rabbits are cuddly,' and 'Keeping them in cages is cruel.'

A myxomatosis epidemic was started artificially with approval by farmers, without consideration for the poor who depended on rabbit meat. After the myxomatosis epidemic had spread, almost all wild rabbits were killed and few wild rabbits were eaten. It was a devastating blow. Eating of white rabbits gradually increased.

I constructed a four tier rabbit hutch with breeding pens, from lathes, wire mesh and plywood. By the time I finished, I had the skills to mend the henhouse.

My rabbit enterprise became a passion for me. When the hundreds of rabbits were healthy and breeding, I was ecstatic.

The rabbits bred like rabbits, more than 100 per doe in a year. It took 28 – 35 days from coitus to birth and then about 3 months for the litter to grow to maturity. Mature does were pregnant most of the time and birthed litters of 12 to 18 kindles. I kept them in an outbuilding, above the farm workshop. They were nervy animals and a sudden noise could panic them. When I walked into the workshop and made a noise, there would be an alarmed thump followed by the thunder of a stampede as they rushed into corners and piled on.

A serious problem was that the pens were infected with coccidiosis, a microorganism transmitted from pen to pen, causing a fatal and cruel gut infection. I fed them medicated feed, or injected them with a treatment and they would still die in pain within 48 hours, no matter how often I disinfected. Penning them on grass to graze was no improvement. If they lived, their metabolisms were so damaged they would never fully recover.

Nietzsche's philosophy (1844-1900) was for an individual to strive using their will-to-power to overcome obstacles that got in their way. I tried very hard to control the rabbit disease. He exhorted us to become 'overmen' as if we could acquire superhuman powers by striving. We didn't learn this in church, for Nietzsche was an atheist. He was also an existentialist, but despite my utmost efforts, the disease shut down my production of rabbits. Whereas I had sent off batches of 40 every two weeks to a packing company, now I had no rabbits well enough to send.

Nietzsche would have wanted me to control the infection, using every bit of will power I could muster. He wanted people to dare to be great, not cringing like slaves. He would want humans to keep rabbits for their meat as a matter of human predation and superior will.

My rabbit enterprise was my passion. When the hundreds of rabbits were healthy and breeding, the enterprise seemed viable. When they were crippled and dying from coccidiosis I was horrified. I supposed the two emotions went together and I wanted to end my hobby but I didn't know how, until I went away to university and left them with my brother. I was thankful he saw the situation demanded solution and culled them.

My breeding of rabbits amounted to a meat factory and it seemed no more cruel than sending cattle and sheep raised in pens for slaughter. The fecundity of the rabbits was exciting. When European rabbits were introduced to Australia, they found the conditions ideal and bred profusely, destroying pastures in competition with cattle and sheep. There had been determined attempts to exterminate them by hunting, by trapping, or with fences. After the myxomatosis virus had done its work, immune rabbit infestation was controlled by other viruses, such as haemorrhagic calicivirus.

Australia had ideal conditions, where rabbits could thrive in the wild and for this reason breeding of rabbits was illegal. Few hunters pursued game. Eating of commercially supplied wild kangaroo meat had adherents and objectors. Game foods were commonly rejected, without their popular niches as delicacies in the UK. Kangaroo meat was available and sold in some supermarkets as 'dog food'. Shooting of ducks and geese meant travelling to the interior where there were floods and droughts. Generally, availability of game meat was irregular and I seldom saw a menu with game on it.

Australians adapted to the shortage of game animals by going without - and by fishing.

CHAPTER 42 CONGER EELS

Local people at the coast in England catch fish from the sea. Australia's coastal waters and rivers are commonly over-fished and depleted of good fish catchable by beach casting. 'Tinny' run-abouts are used to reach good fishing grounds.

Albert, our farm worker, with his family and friends, hunted the rock pools of the foreshore for conger eels. They could be two metres long and ten centimetres in diameter. They were dark above, with white bellies. The meat was white and sweet, unlike the dark muddy meat of freshwater eels. Conger eels spend their entire life in marine waters. Once they reach maturity, which takes between 5 -15 years, they migrate to deep water in the mid-Atlantic to spawn.

Albert's family caught eels in cracks on the rock platform, where they hid between tides. Dogs would bark when they heard them moving and men would use long thin sticks to induce them to leave their hiding places, when they would club them.

McLuhan could have recognised rock platforms as a medium that allowed conger eels to be sorted by size, evading human capture and preserving the fishery.

Skills of building and setting traps were disappearing. A skill in trapping is to imagine the movements of the prey. In catching conger eels, the role of dogs listening for them and enticing them to make an appearance was important. Awareness of these traditional methods could be useful in a survival situation.

According to historian Bruce Pascoe, in his book Dark Emu, fish were trapped by Aborigines in rock pools. Conger eels are found SE of Yamba, New South Wales, to Kangaroo Island, South Australia. Dolphins are reported to have been recruited by humans to assist fishers by rounding-up tuna schools.

Humans in Australia could have developed sea shore conger fishing similar to the UK. Adaptation of the catching methods would be needed for the different structures of rock hiding places.

CHAPTER 43 FISHING

In the UK when I was a boy, I fished for trout in a stream that ran through our farm. It had been stocked with rainbow trout fingerlings by a local landowner, for sport with his friends. He erected a sign: Fishing prohibited. He installed a dam to raise the water level.

Albert and his friends smashed down the dam and caught most of the trout. The farmer on one side told me I could fish from his land. Over a period of several years I fished once or twice a month and always took home several plump fish, which my mother cooked for tea. Rainbow Trout flesh is pink and sweet, with a hint of mud.

In Brisbane, managing our roles in a flood would be ruled by myths from others' experiences. Levi Straus (1908 – 2009) regarded the backbone of community living to be its traditions and myths. The community shared the 'fish' catch. There were many myths about fishing out of season, baits, hooks, lines and taking of undersize fish.

I was an impatient fisher, baiting my hooks with worms, not flies, regarded as unsportsmanlike, by anglers. I didn't wade in the water but sprawled on the bank reading a book. When fish took my bait, sometimes I didn't bait my hook again that day. Fishing interrupted my reading.

Levi Strauss' theory was that every system, including a social system, has a particular structure. The structure of a system determines the position of the whole. It also affects the position of each part of the whole. There was agreement on who could fish and permissible methods. Similarly, there was agreement among the owners of Atrium Apartments about areas to be maintained by the corporate body, about pets and when to evacuate in a flood.

A difficulty with the apartments, as with fishing, was knowing the structure of the social system and being patient with trespassers and bullies.

As a hunter, I was expected to gut and clean fish I brought home. My mother did the cooking, although she didn't eat any of the fish. It could have been part of a myth that females don't eat wild food.

When I lived on an acreage by a river in Australia, the location was an urban suburb. I tried hunting, fishing and growing vegetables, but food could be obtained more easily from supermarkets. There were few fish in the river and the weather was sometimes a drought. When I tried fishing, the fisheries seemed to be depleted. In the Bay, fishing boats had used sonic detectors to find the schools of fish and catch them.

I was without a partner after divorcing Rita. I hadn't seen Vicki for several years and invited her to go deep sea fishing with me from Cairns. We had never been together for such a rugged sport before and my idea was to make new start with her. To my surprise she accepted.

For three days we searched for, hooked and played huge marlin, letting them go when we had had our fun. Vicki showed dogged persistence in pursuit of a quarry and tenacity and strength in the capture.

I enjoyed having Vicki all to myself and we spent a lot of time talking and joking. But she didn't tell me much about herself. There was a man she was seeing but she wouldn't tell me anything about him.

It was a relief when we finally docked. There was a lot of water under the bridge we were on and neither of us was prepared to take the plunge. She had liked catching up but that's all it had been, a catch-up.

CHAPTER 44 ALCOHOLIC BEVERAGES

Australia has a large wine industry. Home-made wine is less popular than in the UK. Many people regarded wine as fruit juice and drink beer. I learned from my mother how to make wine from blackberries and in Australia I made wine from black grapes. I was aiming for a Shiraz taste and had some success. I drank too much wine and eventually quit drinking it.

I was on my way to work on Oxford Street in London. when I was accosted by a person wearing a white coat. He invited me to participate in a beer tasting experiment. He sat opposite me and proffered two glasses of amber fluid which he said was beer.

'Thank you for agreeing to participate, Sir. These two glasses have different beers. Would you sip some of each and answer my questions. Which one do you like best?'

The glass on the left looked like flat beer, with a little foam-like scum on the surface. The glass on the right was filled to the brim with foam, the way I liked my beer. I indicated the one on my right.

'Thank you. Now which one would be more refreshing on a hot day?'

I sipped both but couldn't distinguish them.

'I don't know.'

'Please try again. We can't accept a 'don't know' answer.'

I chose the one on the right again.

'Next, which beer is more nutritious?'

I didn't know and chose the one on the right.

In this way he asked me about 15 questions and I chose the one on the right every time.

'That's all. Thank you,' he said.

I was curious.

'What hypothesis are you testing?'

'We predict that buyers prefer beers with a head of foam. The liquids you have compared are identical, with only a little surfactant added to the one on the right, to cause foaming.'

It was widely believed that foam on beer was good. It was belief inculcated by television advertisements in the many media that the way to advertise beers is to have images of foaming beers being quaffed by celebrities and sports people . This was an example of Marshall McLuhan's theory that 'the medium is the message. His insight was that a medium affects the society in which it plays a role not by the content it delivers, but by its own characteristics. The message of the beer was the way it was served, with lots of foam. Two people drinking beer, typically watched sport in many variations. The foaming image of the beer was iconic and could be addictive.

Quality of the beer was beside the point of drinking choice. I felt cheated that the taste of beer couldn't distinguish a surfactant additive, nor did the foam have any merit. My abstinence would be regarded with suspicion by a pub crowd drinking beer.

It seemed to me that this experiment taught me an important lesson, that the breweries would add chemicals to their products to help sell the drink.

When I was becoming dependant on alcohol, I quit cold turkey. Now I never knowingly drink an alcoholic drink. I regretted ending my experimental making of home-made wines, which was pleasant and could provide gift bottles for family and friends.

Home made wine is easy to make and the small amount made could result from myths promulgated by beer sellers and tax collectors.

CHAPTER 45 HANGING ON

My eyesight, hearing and dentistry had begun to limit me, but I was delaying cataract treatments, hearing aids and extraction of molars.. Ophthalmologists, audiologists and dentists varied widely in their advice about when work should be done. The advice of friends varied considerably and I became convinced that I should delay as long as possible. I took on a mind set which would eke out my competences, avoiding prohibitive deficiencies and keep my independence.

It seemed there were plenty of contexts in which limited hearing and eyesight could be leveraged into expensive remedial treatment or devices. The medium was defective senses and the messages of vision and hearing deficiency were subjective. I was comfortably off in several groups, but keeping up in discussions was reducing my participation and social contact.

The trick to filling my days was to relax and forget the productivity mantra that had kept me at work for so many years. I was often surprised at how many hours there were to fill every day. Earlier, I had always had too many things to do and wanted more time to myself. Now I had more time than I had activities. Writing was my main pastime.

I learned not to trust doctors to investigate any new condition, because they would happily send me for tests when the cause of my complaint was probably their recent treatment. Misdiagnosis could result in unwanted treatment programmes. My ankle swelling was a side effect of a medication, not requiring the lymphoedema programme prescribed, nor the vacuum compression, bandaging and water running. Every medication has a long list of side effects and the doctor had failed to check his screen carefully enough for side effects. With medical effects of most treatments listed on the internet, there was no excuse. The medium was my lymphatic system but the message of a disorder was totally wrong.

An aspect of doctor mistreatment was the tendency to apply two or more treatments for the same condition. They could not know which if any treatment was effective. I suppose they assumed an ineffective treatment could not get in the way. If there was no interference between the treatments, the doctor would be likely to claim a higher rate of success. A doctor could prescribe both bed rest and an antibiotic, as if both could be beneficial, when only one was needed.

Doubling up on treatments had the disadvantage of not finding out how the condition responded to change. When I had a cholesterol problem detected, it was treated with a medication and by drinking less milk. The pills might be ineffective or even have adverse side effects but this might not be discovered. My dieting success would not be revealed. In any case I preferred natural solutions before medications because they were less alien.

Whereas a medical consultation had at one time been conducted sedately in hour-long appointments, now there was the rush and inefficiency of a ten-minute consultation.

Psychiatry was an exception. I would be kept in the waiting room for over an hour by one psychiatrist, who was dishevelled, without apology. Then I heard he had been struck off for debauching his patients rather than repairing their psyches.

CHAPTER 46 OVER-SERVICING

I had assumed care of my health mostly by trial and error. Messages were given by medical or dental practitioners whose remuneration was insufficient to investigate problems thoroughly. The message was usually to keep going back to them, when that could be afforded, at state-subsidised expense, until the condition had been corrected.

Their role was thwarted by my perception that dental and medical practitioners wanted to perform unnecessary procedures, that would reduce my independence and merely take my money.

'I've had a look at those aching teeth,' one dentist said. 'It looks like the nerve has died. They'll have to come out.'

'The ache hasn't been bad,' I said. 'I'd like to wait until it is bad.'

They didn't like it when I wanted a different treatment, but it was part of their code of conduct that the patient was always right.

'Okay. When that happens, make an appointment.'

'Will you show me how to prevent further root decay?'

My dental hygiene lesson was most valuable. He explained how to use a brush, flossing, picksters, an electric toothbrush, and mouth wash, at night daily. My toothache was reduced and I went without yearly checkups. Fewer molars were extracted, with fewer implants and the prolonged use of my teeth was a better solution, over several years. I speculated that if I had been shown how to keep my teeth clean, I would still have a full set of teeth, apart from gaps where teeth had been knocked out playing rugby.

I had changed from my previous dentist because he cleaned my teeth brutally, painfully, with blood everywhere. He held me down, like the Spanish inquisition and scraped excruciatingly.

When my doctor had renewed the prescription I had come for, scanned the results of my blood test, looking for trouble. He found potential for haemochromatosis, excessive iron. There were no symptoms.

'Too much iron can lead to life-threatening conditions, such as liver disease, heart problems and diabetes,' he said.

He sent me for a blood test but there was no sign of any condition.

He puzzled over my low blood pressure, as if this couldn't possibly be normal. He took my blood pressure at every appointment.

'Next you need the follow up bowel scan, to look for any further polyps to be removed.'

I had been reluctant to have another endoscopy, when I protested that their preparation had saturated me with water and I didn't need to have a drip inserted.

They kept me waiting, then overnight, without any reason. In the morning I discharged myself from the hospital.

Now my GP wrote me a letter proposing to insert his finger into my rectum.

I asked for my file to be sent to a different medical practice. The medical practitioners seemed to imagine I was under their control. They did not respect me as the medium for their message.

When I was a school student preparing for exams I developed uncontrolled coughing. Our family doctor sent me to school. He had assumed I was bludging, trying to miss the exam and had sent me to school with pneumonia. I had to withdraw and repeat the exam later, staying on when the other students left school.

In our family, bludging with a medical condition was not allowed. My parents never succumbed to illness and would keep going in a miserable state. When this happened, everyone suffered.

'I wish I never had any children,' my mother would say.

The pretence of a warm loving family was shattered.

A result was that we children were conditioned to keep going when we were ill. It prolonged the illness but developed our self-confidence. Punishment for symptoms assumed imaginary was neglect, or over-servicing. Our bodies, were the health medium, which could generate erratic messages, as McLuhan's theory supposed.

CHAPTER 47 SURVIVAL CAMP

Every year I went with about 60 Year 11 students to Mt Barney in Queensland's Scenic Rim, for a Multistrand Science Survival Camp. Students brought their own tents or shelters and their food for three days. Our bus drove along dirt roads until we reached a favourite bush-walking area.

The idea of the survival camp was to stay alive in the outback, after an accident, without supplies, with simulated hardship conditions. Students would solve the problems of shelter, drinking water and navigating using science methods they had learned. The tasks of survival in the outback medium included building a shelter, water collection, making fire, campfire cooking, orienteering, a night walk and a concert skit. Earlier, the survival camp provided experience of animal trapping, but it threatened wildlife and we now left it out.

The medium of the camp experience was survival. Few students had any previous experience of 'roughing it', or campfire cooking and most joined in the activities with an attitude of 'making do' without the conveniences used by their families on camping forays. The message was that they could enjoy the simplicity and companionship and survive in this environment. McLuhan's theory explained that the hard work was not pointless and not too difficult. Survival methods worked.

Survival in modern times has benefitted by developments in communications, vehicular transport and provisions for nutrition. In 1861 the Burke and Wills expedition, crossing the continent from Melbourne to the Gulf of Carpentaria, was confounded by starvation, heat, pack animal exhaustion and scurvy. The destinations changed, the routes were remote, the explorers split into three groups, the leaders died, the horses and camels expired without food and water and a party was attacked repeatedly by Aborigines. With modern conveniences the expedition would probably have succeeded.

Many of my students 'found' themselves during our 'survival' camp, dividing sometimes into female or male roles and participating in activities with gender expectations different from those set at home. The camp was a welcome change, allowing them to do whatever activities interested them.

I showed them how to dig a pit, fill it with vegetation and cover it with a clear plastic sheet. The vegetation warmed up and transpired moisture, which condensed under the plastic and run down the sheet to a low point, where it dripped into a collecting container. The amount of water collected was small, but it could be life-saving, producing more if the pit was used for urination. The water would be better drinking quality than that drained from a car radiator

To make fire, I provided a bow and drill, enabling a person to saw with the bow like a fiddler, spinning the drill. The point of the drill was held in a hole in a piece of wood covered with tinder. Friction of the wooden drill against the wood was sufficient to ignite the tinder. Pressing on the end with your hand could cause blisters, unless you held the drill in a glass spice jar.

Orienteering navigated a course of several kilometres, in rocky terrain or forest, visiting checkpoints on a map. Students learned to read a contour map and take bearings with a compass, without a GPS.

The night walk under the stars introduced students to features of the night sky, such as phases of the Moon, the constellations, rotation of the night sky and revolution in the annual cycle. When I had taught them how to frame the night sky, students made their own observations locating and naming celestial objects with star maps.

On the last evening, students were required to entertain the group. They could put on a skit they had made up, or do some other activity. A few found it difficult to act in front of the group, never having done this before. They were allowed to read a poem and no-one was harmfully embarrassed.

The philosophy of the Survival Camp was application of science to solving simulated problems of survival. Marshall McLuhan's philosophy was prominent in the message of determination, forethought and adaptation to the outback medium.

CHAPTER 48 ARTIFICIAL SELECTION

I taught at a school which offered studies in agriculture and many of the students lived on properties with cattle. The education was not unlike a school in rural England. Although schools in Australia and England were physically and linguistically far apart, philosophically and ethically they were close.

Grazing cattle in Australia were different UK cattle. Apart from a few breeds such as Droughtmaster that could resist droughts, Australian cattle harvested plants growing in the bush and stored them as meat on the hoof, until they were slaughtered to supply urban consumers. Every year or two, there was a drought and then the herds were without feed or water and had to be culled.

I was intrigued how Australian animals had evolved by artificial selection. Spoken evaluations were explained by Saussure's theory that local languages are structured systems of signs that derived meaning from their relationships to one another, rather than from individual utterances. When the adjudicators of the animal judging competition talked, their reasoning was stilted and at first I did not understand it. I don't think they wanted me to know their ideas, in case they were controversial. Saussure's idea was that talk was often like that, restricted to those who were involved.

In the UK, farmers in our community had selected animals for centuries. Farmers with a good commercial eye for animals prospered. Saussure (1857 - 1913) explained the role of language and other sign systems for communicating the knowledge within communities such as farmers. They had their own language, with a rich local vocabulary. Outsiders could have great difficulty adapting. For example, the protocols used to negotiate repair of damage by the hunt to farm fences and gates was complex. In Australia occupation groups such as miners had their own languages. I had to learn meanings as an outsider, rather than being raised with them from childhood.

Breeders of commercial dairy and beef animals had a language of attributes and deficiencies which they used to shape their animals, year after year, wanting to develop their own 'types' or tropes to sell at a premium. This was artificial selection.

David Suzuki, a Canadian space scientist, tells a story about the evolution by artificial selection of the Samurai crab in the waters of Japan. Japanese fisherman, who have plundered these waters for thousands of years, would throw back any crab caught in their net if its carapace resembled the scowling face of a samurai. Local fishermen selected the best likenesses to preserve the spirits and threw them back, uncannily shaping the images on their shells to resemble samurai warriors. They believe that these crabs are reincarnations of the fierce samurai defeated at the naval Battle of Dan-no-ura. Tradition has it that all the warriors were slain or drowned and their spirits survive in effigy on the carapaces of crabs.

Livestock breeders likewise have images of animal appearance etched in their minds that they look for when they select animals for breeding. The selection processes apply the experience of selectors, in the same way as the fishermen who select samurai crabs. Various aspects are selected, such as sizes of body parts, facial appearance, apparent intelligence and educational ability. Saussure's theory was that the linguistic system in each individual's brain is constructed from experience. This would explain how livestock breeders could develop new types intuitively without conscious design. It explains how new fashionable breeds came into existence.

In farm animals and young humans, the criteria for favourable selection are well known. Unusual size, odd features, appendages, extra limbs, protuberances, discoloration and asymmetries are often penalised by normative standards, although new types sometimes get through. For example the Brahman's hump had evolved over time to help the animal survive in hot, arid conditions. It is made up of tissue that stores water.

Young men and women are most carefully scrutinised when they reach breeding age, to discover any conditions that could be genetic and exacerbated in their offspring..

I didn't remain interested in livestock for long. I have mentioned the deliberate breeding outcomes with livestock to illustrate how humans shape their progeny when they select their mates. The horrid disease in my rabbits put me off animal husbandry and my attention turned to machinery and crops.

CHAPTER 49 ASTRONOMY NIGHT

Students who a year earlier had gone on the night walk at the Survival Camp, pitched their tents in the grounds of a local school in the country, where there was no artificial lighting. I had arranged that members of a local astronomy club would bring telescopes and demonstrate them in an all-night vigil. Some of the telescopes were large, 400 mm diameter and 3 metres long, mounted on trailers.

Students who had no special scientific interest, became captivated by the majesty and enormity of the night sky. The girls and boys, in Year 12, found the darkness comfortable and talked more than they usually did in social situations. They were more humble than usual and concerned about the meaning of the universe and its future, rather than sticking to egocentric preoccupations.

Some girls and boys paired off. They may not have had the anonymity or opportunity to do so earlier, during their years at school together.

McLuhan (1964) suggested that all media, all technologies, are merely extensions of our bodies or our psyches. Contrary to expectations, even the most powerful telescope was unable to obtain a view with details of even the largest and closest stars. Nevertheless, the students focussed the telescopes on distant objects. McLuhan's message would be the distance to the objects from the Earth's rotating viewing platform. The medium of an optical telescope provided a viewing platform for stunning observations of the largest close objects, such as the Rings of Saturn. They discovered that the observer's position changed so fast and the objects were so far away, that great care was needed to focus on them. The main difficulty was the diurnal rotation of the Earth and revolution of the night sky with the seasons. The message of the telescope observations was tentative but revealed real objects. Humans' places in the universe were real and extraordinary.

Students were interested in space travel and colonisation of Mars. When they realised the distances and travel times, they concluded that emigration could possibly become feasible in the not too distant future.

CHAPTER 50 NUCLEAR POWER

Human consequences of the bombs dropped on Hiroshima and Nagasaki had been suppressed at first, but reports of the effects on victims were gradually revealed. They were horrific, with people incinerated and 'melted', dying in extreme pain. Blast damage, heat radiation, radiation sickness and fallout sickness had immediate effects but the medical effects were insidious and sometimes were not discovered until decades later.

The UK's nuclear power stations were built in the 1950s and 1960s, possibly as a political response to militancy of coal workers. Foucault expected nuclear power to develop in reaction to investment imperatives of powerful stakeholders. There was an anti-nuclear movement fearful of further prospects for nuclear war. There was another round of approvals when the coal miners tried to have their own way with Prime Minister Margaret Thatcher. It was a bitter uprising and the miners lost. Foucault's theories primarily addressed the relationships between power versus knowledge and liberty, and he analysed how they are used as a form of social control through multiple institutions.

A less kind interpretation of the UK nuclear power programme the philosophy of Albert Camus. At the heart of Camus' philosophy was the concept of the absurd, which arises from the conflict between the human desire for significance, order, and clarity on one hand, and the silent, irrational, and indifferent world on the other. The power stations were very expensive and various commentators remarked on their absurdity.

A new 3.3 GW nuclear power station, Hinkley A, started up beside our farm in 1965. The site had been chosen for its sea water cooling at a location remote from urban populations in natural surroundings unvisited except by fox hunters, bird watchers and shore fishers. A second B station followed in 1976. In 1986 a reactor exploded at Chernobyl power station in the Ukraine. Radioactive fall-out was detected as far away as Sweden and Ireland.

After another interval of 30 years, construction of a third C station began in 2017. The stations were opposed at first by nuclear disarmament protesters and later by environmental activists. Supporters included residents of local villages and workers from Bridgwater, employed during the construction and operating phases.

I worked as a vacation student in 1964 at Hinkley Point A in the chemistry laboratory, monitoring radioactive emissions in the environment and various effluents. I recall there was some radioactivity in the residues extracted from the wind on 'tacky shades' but never enough for a leak to be assumed. My family farmed up to the station boundary and I have never heard of any pollution effects. Livestock abortions and birth deformities continued as usual on farms. They were never attributed to radioactive emissions.

Station 'A' was decommissioned in 2000 and B station ceased operation in 2022. Their sites were encased in concrete, forever excised from human occupation. Foucault's theory could interpret these power stations as instruments of social control, by their concentration of power versus knowledge and liberty.

My purpose here is to remark effects of nuclear technology now being considered for installation in Australia. No doubt the design and safety of the reactors would have improved, but the technology would be essentially the same. Uranium fuel rods were brought from Sellarfield in Northumbria, by heavy road transport in one or two deliveries per year. Transporting uranium fuel to Australia would be hazardous.

Health threatening danger to workforces exposed at nuclear power stations is real and not well understood. For my job in the chemistry laboratory, I was required to wear a film badge on my lapel, which when developed with photochemicals, gave a visible record of the amount of radiation I had received. My exposure was within safety limits. If a worker was over-exposed, he would be moved to a safe position so as not to overload his immune system. Species of radioactive particle could vary and individual reactions varied. Nuclear safety is not as simple as donning a safety helmet.

Spent fuel rods were allowed to 'cool' down until they would be returned to Sellarfield for reprocessing. The amount of material involved was small but highly dangerous if released. Careful precautions were observed to guard against collisions with railway trains or bridges, which could release radioactive material. The waste was carried in a thick-walled heavy lead container ominously referred to as 'the coffin'.

Construction of the 'C' station could cost 36 billion in 2015 prices.

I doubt this enormous cost would be cheaper than alternatives reckoned to be more environment friendly, such as renewable energy.

Reduced demand for electricity should be more prominent in energy planning. Both England and Australia have high per capita electricity consumption with availability a luxury rather than a necessity in many instances. In my view the retreat from fossil fuels is unwarranted and overdone. The allocation of blame to carbon dioxide for climate disasters is exaggerated and the cost of withdrawal from fossil fuels is enormous with success uncertain.

Supposing carbon dioxide really causes significant global warming, responsibility for climate warming and sea level rise depends on how far away emissions are, as well as on quantity of emissions. Emissions decline in significance and retention in the atmosphere, with long distances. Emissions from remote and sparsely populated Australia are less to blame for climate change in Europe than are emissions penetrating from intensely populated nearby European neighbours.

Students were required to take a position, for or against, a new nuclear station. Their views divided into would-be engineers and would-be environmentalists. There was little compromise between the two groups, nor much interest in investigating the realities. It seemed to be an emotive division, in which students depended on outside experience or an authority for their opinions.

During the Covid 19 pandemic, social distancing in West End, Australia, was not unlike the plague in the fictional French Algerian city of Oran, reported by philosopher Albert Camus. Pandemic precautions were like those adopted against Covid. The irony of the story is that citizens of Oran become prisoners of the plague when their city fell under total quarantine, but it is questionable whether they were really 'free' before the plague. Resistance against government controls occurred. Albert Camus' story is an absurdist satire revealing the technology that the government used to control Covid had not advanced much in 80 years: in his story city-wide quarantine was contemplated..

It seems ironic that the benefits of a nuclear power strategy in Australia have been lampooned as absurd, when the need for it is so controversial.

A nuclear conflict or accident would result in casualties and restrictions not unlike Covid 19. The effects could be catastrophic and the government should adopt nuclear power as a last resort. Emissions from reactor accidents could be fatal, dwarfing carbon emissions with fatalities rather than climate discomfort.

CHAPTER 51 QUANTOCK PONIES

The Quantock Hills west of Bridgwater in Somerset, consist of heathland, oak woodlands, ancient parklands and agricultural land. It is an area of outstanding beauty and used for recreation, wild deer and hill ponies.

Hill ponies owned by local people graze the common land, by right. The various herds may number several hundred ponies in total. Ownership of grazing rights may entail obligations for mending fences, cattle grids and gates.

Although hill ponies have grazed the Quantock Hills for hundreds of years, there have been incursions into the natural domain, for example during WWII some of the heath was ploughed and seeded with grass.

Karl Popper wrote a philosophical book (1944) called the poverty of historicism. In 1972 he wrote a book of essays Objective Knowledge. Changes in the number of ponies from year to year can be presented as hypotheses, able to be refuted. An hypothesis is an educated guess of an outcome. His method can be used for considering change in owners' holdings by deducing the numbers of mares and foals by systematic refutation of hypotheses.

In September, riders muster the pony herd. It is a magnificent sight, thundering down the main road into the village of Nether Stowey, where they are corralled and ponies separated to be sold in Bridgwater's annual horse fair. Ponies too young to be sold are left with their mothers and put back on the hills for another year.

When I was 14 I was given a hill pony by my father. My pony was half-Arabian, from a pure-bred stallion owned by one of the commoners. I was without riding experience and we broke each other in. He was a wonderful horse and I became very fond of him.

The main interest in ponies is by females. Girls like to control a large and strong animal, with patience and kindness. A horse could be a girl's surrogate man to control. Boys are less gentle and impatient to dominate their mount, requiring it to perform exactly the behaviour they want, with rougher control.

The hill ponies are a thriving community. Foucault would have observed the balance of power between the common holders and ponies and how knowledge and liberty form a stable social control.

When wild terrain and its animal population survives human incursions and thrives, as do the Quantock hill ponies, it is a source of inspiration for those living nearby and caring for the animals. Australia is fortunate to have forest country with wild hill ponies called brumbies, where common land is being preserved.

CHAPTER 52 WATER DIVINING

I had trained as a petroleum reservoir engineer. When we built on our acreage south of Brisbane, there was no reticulated water supply. It was on the banks of the Logan River but it was a steep climb down to the water, except when it flooded and overflowed its banks.

Most people relied on water from their roofs and installed large tanks.

I inquired about drilling a bore. A neighbour supplied me with the phone number of a water diviner who had located a bore which supplied his house. When I phoned the diviner, he asked where my house was situated.

I told him it was on the next block to the well he had divined.

'Oh, there,' he said. 'I'm not going to work there again! It's too difficult. Divining that bore put me in hospital.'

The diviner's experience conflicted with my experience that underground water could be found at most locations if you drilled deep enough. The rock outcropping locally was unconsolidated sandstone and I predicted water would flow into bores without divine intervention. The uncertainty was depth to the water table. My neighbour's water had been found by the diviner at 100 feet. He told me how he had divined it.

'I walked along lines 40 metres apart in a grid, holding a Y-shaped piece of wire in front of me,' he told me. 'When it twisted and pointed downwards, that was where we drilled and found water.' Water divining seemed to be arduous but the medical effects were uncertain. The role of the diviner and his belief in the Divine puzzled me, but I have come across other situations where God's guidance is invoked. I have an unusual knowledge of waterways in deposition of sandstones and I suppose some people prefer to trust in God.

Karl Popper would have investigated sites where water had been found by drilling and compared evidence with other sites where water had been found by divining. I didn't have enough data to decide either way. I had no reason to believe divining could find water. In any case, the diviner had refused to divine a new well on my land.

I resorted to my hypothesis that if you drill, you will come to water.

Without more ado, I picked a convenient location close to my house tank and engaged a driller. He roared down to 100 feet with dust and chips blowing from the hole.

When he reached 100 feet deep, I told him to stop.

'Pull out,' I said to him. 'I can't afford to go deeper.'

'I'll shout you a joint,' he said and attached another length of pipe to the drill string.

When he reached full depth and was pulling back out, water gurgled out of the hole.

'There it is,' he said.

'It's a bit salty,' I said tasting it.

'You had better get it tested,' said Rita.

I checked it with the school's scientific salinity meter.

'It's okay for cattle and sheep.'

'You had better get it tested,' said Rita, as usual pessimistic and persistent.

'What if the test shows it's unfit for us? What will we do?'

I began pumping water from the river into the tank, topping up from the bore when the tank was low. We drank water from that bore for 20 years without any problems.

People who have towns water have a good thing going. We never had enough water for long showers, for watering the lawn or for growing fruit trees. But we got by. It's the same problem as with reticulated electricity. When it is connected, you use a lot. People can do without it most of the time. Most consumption is unnecessary.

When we lived on bore water from our tank, we were careful with showering and let the lawn fend for itself. Plants struggled and we envied city dwellers with their irrigation systems. They suffered in the drought of 2001 to 2009, when Brisbane residents' consumption of water fell from 350 litres per person per day to 130 litres per day. Most people economised voluntarily and they saved enough to prevent the dam from emptying.

CHAPTER 53 ENERGY SUPPLY

It is difficult to know how much energy is used by domestic electrical appliances. I had thought that an air conditioner would use more electricity than any other appliance, so I was reluctant to use mine, unless it was uncomfortably warm.

When the local City Council installed in my home a Smart Energy Monitor, I thought my days guessing electricity use were over. Its purpose was to help me reduce my electricity demand. It measured energy use of each appliance and calculated its cost per hour. The dishwasher, stove, washing machine, fridge and oven, plus lighting, together made up the total cost.

The air conditioner was much cheaper to use than I expected and I began to turn it on more often. The Smart Energy Monitor had increased my electricity demand, opposite to the decrease foretold by the electricity authority.

It was a 'paradigm shift' to devolve control of electricity use to the monitor's cost per appliance, as a fundamental change in approach or in underlying assumptions identified by Kuhn (1822–1990). More recently, there has been a paradigm shift from fossil fuels to renewable energy and the change is being paid for by electricity consumers.

After the monitor was installed, I asked my electricity supplier to install a Smart Meter, which has tariffs that vary between off-peak, shoulder and peak times. I now use the oven, washing machine, tumble drier and dishwasher between 10pm and 7am. My electricity bill seemed to have decreased. Public energy demand could be reduced hugely if smart meters offer sufficient incentives to consumers.

There were news stories about shutting down coal stations and replacement of electricity supply by renewables. Wind and solar electricity were available around midday and coal stations could provide back-up at some other times. If I bought an electric car it could reduce emissions and use renewable energy. It was not evident that the substitution would reduce my electricity cost. Electricity would become more expensive.

Australians used a lot of electricity in 2021, with national consumption of 9,143 kWh/year compared with Norway's 24,182 kWh/year and India's 1,025 kWh/year. Transitioning of electricity supply could reduce Australia's consumption greatly. Halving of personal consumption, as with water under drought conditions, is possible but people may be unwilling to reduce to half their usage because of severe cost penalties. If Australians would use less electricity, Indians should be able to use more for essential purposes provided they were allowed to generate if from fossil fuels.

PART 5: ADVENTURES

Australians use much of their high energy consumption in foreign travel. During the three years I lived in Canada, I visited various countries and had experiences that satiated my interest in adventurous travel. Here I have recorded the enjoyment I experienced from performing several journeys that I would not repeat because they could not be surpassed. I substituted exploration in sport, metaphysics, climate science and climate politics having post-modern philosophies with hidden meanings requiring to be teased out.

CHAPTER 54 STOPPING WITHOUT BRAKES

I found my work in Canada in my first job frustrating and I sought excitement playing rugby: skiing, flying and partying. My position in the herd at work was undistinguished and I had to be content with wild rugby games and rugby club parties.

I bought a 1957 Jaguar Mk VIII, 3.4 Litre, inline 6 cylinder. It was a large saloon model, a rounded upright silver car in which diplomats had ridden in luxury. It featured walnut hinged tables in the back seat, ideal for going to the races or to drive-in movies.

Girls were impressed by my car and enjoyed going to drive-ins in it, sitting in the back seats and waving languidly to crowds we passed. For the harsh winters, it lacked heating. Unless the engine was kept warm all night, it wouldn't start.

Unfortunately the footbrake had broken. I was unable to obtain a replacement in Canada for the brake master cylinder. It was virtually undrivable, difficult to stop because it was a heavy car. There were a few ways of operating the car that enabled it to be stopped by the disabled brakes. I learned to slow down by stemming across its trajectory, as one does on skis by turning sideways to check momentum. My philosophy was to convert the car's energy into tyre heat. I refined my technique considering the best ways to dissipate the kinetic energy of the car, by law abiding and safety conscious methods. In a straight run downhill, without an intersection, I weaved with tyres howling. To avoid traffic lights, I sometimes turned abruptly on to a side road.

I analysed stopping situations carefully to find the best ways to bring the car to a halt. I evaded private danger and enjoyed the excitement. But there was no doubt that my ways of stopping were dangerous and I became ultra cautious. I had the advantage of understanding of physics and how to minimise the risks I took. I drove the car regularly for several months without brakes. I was fortunate not to have an accident.

Eventually I obtained a brake master cylinder and fitted it. Driving the sedate car became less fun.

CHAPTER 55 ACORN BOUTIQUE

In search of adventure, I quit my job in Canada and set off to drive to Toronto. In Saskatchewan, I visited the boutique I had started with a friend two years previously when we were both posted by our company to Regina. He was married. I had been the best man at their wedding in England.

They had relatives in London who supplied them with women's fashions, mini-skirts and hot-pants. We leased a store in a shopping mall near the city centre and air-freighted a containerful of garments. We sold this 'Carnaby Street gear' at a large mark-up, to prairie farmers' wives when they came to town to spend their grain cheques.

The boutique was a success but earned less than our jobs with the oil company. We learned that buyers would ignore a few garments unless we displayed them in the front window with a sign: SALE 50% OFF. Then we quadrupled the selling price. Most items sold quickly.

When they transferred us to other regional offices, we sold the business at a large profit.

I called in at the shop on my journey east. I found that the new owners were losing money. They hadn't renovated the business and didn't have reliable fashion suppliers. A boutique has to be renewed frequently to maintain a trendy image.

The boutique enterprise had involved innovation in fashion retailing. We had made a fundamental change in underlying assumptions from traditional women's wear. This was Kuhn (1922–1996)'s paradigm shift away from solely progressing in a linear and continuous way. We had been fortunate to commence the business when we did and to sell it when we did. Retailing of fashions was notorious for becoming outdated.

We could have extended our adventure to open a chain of boutiques across Canada, but we knew it took attention and effort to run a boutique profitably. Nor did we know how to hire and motivate store managers. It seemed best to stick to our jobs with the oil company.

CHAPTER 56 DRIVING TO PANAMA

I drove through America from Chicago to Kentucky and down to Texas, then into Mexico and along the Pan-American highway to Panama. I sold my car then flew to Bogota and took buses around South America, eventually returning to England.

The tedium of driving large distances was relieved by picking up hitch hikers and by avoiding huge potholes in the road. I spent three months crossing Mexico, to Acapulco and visiting the pyramids in Yucatan and on down to Belize.

In Belize I had found myself staying in a house with several dope smoking hitchhikers. I was shaken down by a cool black Dude with dreads, from New York.

'You got grass?' he demanded.

I had in my car a kilogram brick I had bought in Acapulco. It was good stuff and I wanted to keep it. I didn't answer but he pulled out a knife and aimed where he would stick it in me.

'I've a kilo,' I admitted.

'Get it,' he ordered meanly.

I fetched it from my car and gave it to him.

He took it all. I figured it wasn't worth dying for.

He skilfully rolled me a dozen joints with one hand.

I took them and left for Guatemala.

It was the last time I carried drugs in any quantity.

This exchange did not trifle with Derrida's binary opposition. The spade had been in a strong position to negotiate with me and had got what he wanted almost effortlessly. After he unsheathed his knife, my opposition was token.

Derrida (1930s–2004) sought not only to impose an interpretation in the present, but also sought transcendental signifieds – concepts which overarched past and future, near and far, similar and dissimilar. He was most celebrated as the principal philosopher exponent of deconstruction, a term he coined for the critical examination of the fundamental conceptual distinctions, or 'oppositions,' inherent in Western philosophy since the time of the ancient Greeks. His deconstruction of the meaning of my presence was masterly. I was a traveller when I was on the road. At other times I was stopped, opposed by the spade.

The dissolution of objective meaning infects every concept and had a significant impact on our conception of the world and of ourselves. Metaphysical concepts have been defined by opposition and cannot be articulated independently. For instance, 'subject' implies 'objects', 'self' implies 'other', substance implies 'quality'; and so on. My 'having' grass implied he could 'take it' from me.

My car was taken from me, at an unfairly low price, in Panama, under similar circumstances. It was a lawless place.

A dealer made me an offer I couldn't refuse. Derrida would deconstruct my situation that I was stuck with a car that I could sell only at a low price, giving a hefty bribe. I was glad to have sold it. At every border crossing, I had been targeted by officials to make extortive payments. The car had become a millstone around my neck and it was a relief to be rid of it.

CHAPTER 57 SERENGHETTI BALLOON SAFARI

I had met Cynthia by online dating. She was an activist and led a group who sought preservation of an historic building in Brisbane. Yungaba Migrant Reception Centre had been sold by the State Government for redevelopment by a private developer who proposed to build a block of several hundred apartments and convert the old building into luxury flats.

Cynthia led a group who opposed the State Government's disposal of the site. She wanted to convert the old building into an emigration museum to commemorate the role emigration had played in development of Queensland.

Cynthia was familiar with the legislation regulating sale of public property. I joined in with her group, planning protest actions and taking our opposition to the Environmental Court. By seeing Cynthia socially and through my involvement in her Yungaba Action Group, I got to know her well.

When Tegan invited me to visit her in Kenya, I considered asking Vicki to come with me on a visit to Serengeti Game Park where we would observe the annual wildebeest migration. We could visit Tegan in Nairobi, where she was employed supplying mosquito control equipment such as bed nets to African governments. It was an opportunity to be with Vicki and could even lead to a relationship at last. But Tegan hardly knew Vicki and wanted Cynthia to come. I had been with Cynthia for several years and it didn't seem right to go with Vicki behind her back. So, I took Cynthia, and Vicki wasn't asked.

Hanging in a huge basket from an enormous hot air balloon, we flew across the main migration artery. It was a jaw dropping view, stretching from horizon to horizon, the blackness of the animals spread out like a river flooding the plains below us, narrowing at river crossings to defiles attended by crocodiles. We watched the Big Five: Elephants, Lions, Leopard, Rhino and Cape buffalo intermingled with herds of zebra, antelope, giraffes and chetahs, moving in the boundless tide of wildebeests.

I was intrigued by the herds of zebra mingling with the wildebeest, stalked by lions. Wildebeest eyesight is poor, so they stay near zebra who have excellent vision. Conversely, Wildebeest can smell lions well, whereas zebras' smelling is not so good. These animals complemented each other's defensive skills. Other species, such as hippos, were not part of the main migration.

DeBord's theory of The Spectacle described the human audience who had paid to watch the wildebeest migration. It was wonderful entertainment and we could see how it had survived. Our balloon was not intrusive as we alighted for refreshments served by ground crews. The fascination of the annual migration was simply mesmerising and would keep people paying, for more flights, with political votes as well as monetization. I enjoyed a wonderful holiday with Cynthia. We continued to live apart and when the river flooded I evacuated from my place to live with her for a couple of weeks. Cleaning up was stressful and Cynthia was an archivist with experience of rescuing books. We were both set in our ways and Cynthia was content to adopt Kierkegard's duality. I was an intractable agnostic and we separated when grew restless for a change.

CHAPTER 58 MEKONG RIVER JOURNEY

I visited Tegan in Vietnam. We took a bus from Vietnam through neighbouring Laos and then down the vast Mekong River in an airboat. We hurtled through rapids and around rocks.

Baudrillard (1929 – 2007) claimed that current society had replaced all reality and meaning with symbols and signs, and that human experience is a simulation of reality. Our riverboat excursion seemed to be an aggregation of modern separate experiences rather than an integrated tradition. Like the hot air balloon journey across the Serengeti, the airboat journey over the Mekong had an important element of the unreal. The Mekong was an essential element in the spectacle of Vietnam, attracting business people and tourists.

'Philosopher Jean Baudrillard's theory is that unless something can be simulated, it cannot become real,' I said. 'The airboat journey was fast, too brief for me to understand and remember much. The ride was wild and exciting and because it could not be simulated, unreal. But the Mekong experience was real enough.'

We returned to Hanoi in time to enjoy the February Tet and Kumquat festivals. The roads were clogged with motor bikes carrying cumquat trees, conical and green with shiny orange fruits, like Christmas Tree decorations. The cumquats had been grown in pots indoors, providing a type of air-conditioning in the hot Vietnamese summer. My hotel lobby had a boulevard of pristine cumquat trees, removing hot air and heat. The Vietnamese response to summer heat was to adapt to it, providing shade and cool air by the transpiration of the trees. Besides the shade of the trees, cumquats are eaten peel and all, or used to make delicious cumquat marmalade.

CHAPTER 59 POLE VAULTING

The training of Megan, a self-coached pole vaulter, is described in my book *Turkeys not Bees* (2022).

She used Heidegger's method to record the phenomena of her performances, superimposing camera observations and analyses on a digital model, using the simulation to suggest improvements.

Heidegger's analysis objectifies the existential performance while excluding outside experience. He inverts Cartesian concepts that elaborate technique rather than developing an integrated solution to each attempt.

The sponsors carefully concerted the spectacle of her performances for audience enjoyment and ticket sales. Pole vaulting encouraged audiences to fantasize.

Jean Baudrillard's 'Simulation and Simulacra' explored the idea of a simulated world where the distinction between illusion and reality is lost. Field athletics performances are spectacles with inexpert audiences and obscure techniques.

'Simulation is no longer that of a territory, a referential being, or a substance. It is the generation by models of performance without origin or reality: a hyperreal.'

Megan's pole vaults had the quality of an elaborate fantasy. Her performances were highly rehearsed and it was difficult for spectators to understand the difficulties except by showing the heights achieved in relation to records.

She self-coached her practice jumps, but was coached for strength, fitness and concentration. She embraced the flow technique used by endurance athletes and was coached in Zen to refine her concentration.

CHAPTER 60 GOVERNMENT OVERREACH

My book *Nanny State* (2024) reveals the view of a Canadian that government in Australia exceeds wants of many citizens.

'Australia is becoming the world's dumbest nation . . . (because of) the removal of personal responsibility and the increase in the number and scope of health and safety laws,' Tyler Brule, Monocle , 2015.

'There is a fine line between a state that supports and one that suffocates. What makes socialism dangerous is not its intent but its effect: it treats disparity as injustice, success as exploitation and liberty as an obstacle to equality.'

Debord explains government overreach as subscribed to by audiences paying to watch an absorbing spectacle. The audiences are alienated from their work and have their leisure planned. Besides monetary payments for their audience experience, the support of those who can vote is sought by governments and corporations having democratic input.

I met Kathy at the distance education school where I was a science teacher and she was implementing the national English curriculum. I taught classes of students with science lessons I prepared using online systems such as Powerpoint. She trained teachers to deliver English lessons with approved contents and processes.

Emphases in English teaching were an old chestnut and there was always controversy. A frequent view was that the State was overreaching in making too many demands on students and their teachers.

Kathy coordinated lesson preparation by English teachers. Their lessons were trialled at various schools statewide and Kathy would visit schools to get feedback from parents.

Several schools told her that the word 'fuck' in the students' reader was inappropriate. She flew to the schools and met with parents and teachers.

'There wasn't much agreement. Her main argument was that students should be exposed to language in current everyday use. Parents did not dispute that 'Fuck' was in current use at workplaces and in most media. They argued that its use was in poor taste, as emotive and crude talk. They highlighted the need for students to learn more expressive communication.'

'The English used in our textbooks finds its way into family vocabularies and dramas,' she told me. 'New experiences are resented. Parents acknowledge there has been language change, but most of them resent it. We can see this in their desire to preserve Shakespeare's language.'

Parents harked back to traditional standards of swearing in texts and wanted Kathy's reader cancelled despite it having been purchased.

'The complaint was a microcosm of parents' reversion to former language restrictions, as if English content should be static,' Kathy told me.

Kathy was annoyed but there was no alternative.

It was an example of government overreach in education, health, business, sport and public control. Government response to people's wants is usually a plan and there are so many overlapping plans that standards are difficult to distinguish, with much that is superfluous and fantasy.

The experience of overreach is explained by Baudrillard as simulated and hyperreal.

The place of racy language in the senior English curriculum had been debated through many iterations, without resolution. I kept clear and supported Kathy when I could. The reversion to earlier points of view allowed fantasies in. Parents seemed to consider new language in a burble of unreal voices. It made me wonder how the issue had been able to be skirted previously.

Planning in Australia is done by governments or by large corporations in Canberra or in state capitals. School syllabuses dictate the minutiae of what can be presented in classrooms. Keeping the content current is difficult. Planning can enact or thwart legislation.

People reacted against change and Kathy's task to modernise the English syllabus was very difficult. She became cynical and dictatorial. I was unsympathetic and we parted.

CHAPTER 61 FLOW

This section is from Chapter 45 of my book *Time is Gold*. It reveals the psychological theory of 'flow', a technique published by Mihaly Csikszentmihalyi, 1990 and adopted by many runners and performers. I was interested in training athletes in flow for higher achievement.

My story is about a marathon runner I coached called Maxi. She claimed that when she ran in a psychological state known as 'flow', she could perform faster than opponents.
'Maxi has run 2h25,' I said. 'Let's look at how she finishes in front. In Brisbane, Maxi ran 'in flow' for several intervals. Could she run 'in flow' for more of the race?'
'Is that the same as being 'in the zone'?' asked Blake.
'Yes.'
'Are we sure it's a real effect?' said Stan, her father, sceptically.
'It is contentious but I'm convinced it has helped Maxi,' Alice said.
'I've experienced flow at my desk,' I said, 'but it may not be the same as Maxi's flow.'
'Maxi, could you tell us about your experiences in-flow?' said Derek.
'Runners call it 'in flow',' she said. 'I've been practicing it with Dr Minami, although she refers to it as 'It.''
'Dr Minami wants flow to be a Zen experience.'
'The psychologist Mihaly calls it 'flow' and runners call it 'in the zone' or 'runners' high', said Alice. 'No-one so far has explained exactly how it improves performance.'

'This is how,' said Maxi. 'Two weeks ago in the Brisbane Marathon I was 'in flow' from about 5 kilometres out to 15 kilometres.'

'Did it feel good?' I asked.

'Yes, a sort of stoned ultra-realism.'

'What happened.'

'I had a fast start. I concentrated on achieving my target rate. I didn't acknowledge the pain and cruised 'in flow' until about 15 kilometres. Then I was uncomfortable and got thrown out of 'flow'. After that I was doing it tough. Near the end I gave it everything I had, took the lead and stayed there.'

'Do you think your time in 'flow' helped you?' I said.

'It was comfortable and enjoyable.'

'I have noticed when you are totally engaged, in flow, in training runs, you seem to speed up,' I said. 'It's not scientific, but enough to keep us believing in it.'

'Do psychologists have any ideas how flow works, Alice?' I asked. It was her expertise.

'Have you ever been absorbed in something you like doing, using your skills, with all your attention taken and before you know it, several hours have whizzed past?' said Alice. 'You were 'in flow'. Most of us experience it in our work, recreation or hobby, from time to time.'

'Like meditation?'

'It is a type of meditation,' said Alice. 'It's effortless and absorbing, enabling enjoyable timeless concentration, freeing up attention and energy to obtain more achievement. Mihaly called it 'optimal experience'. It's a sort of deep immersion characterised by automaticity. Self-consciousness disappears and the person's sense of time becomes distorted.

'Identical regular events, like a runner's striding, can seem predictable and boring but 'in flow' they're not. Waiting for the kettle to boil can seem interminable but time spent chatting with a celebrity can flash past.'

'Is it a type of play?'

'Yes. You're playing when you lose yourself in what you're doing, forgetting yourself and forgetting time. You're not in it for a reward. You get rid of bottled up feelings, feel energetic, relaxed and satisfied.'

'Is flow a mind trip, like a rush or intoxication?' asked Blake.

'When an effect is confused with its cause, it is the fallacy: 'post hoc ergo propter hoc'' I said. 'The notion that flow induces high performance could be a tautology, because they occur simultaneously.'

'It's not a tautology,' Alice said. 'Being 'in flow' and performing well are not the same thing. Being 'in flow' is a definite psychological condition.'

'You mean there's an organic change in the person when in flow?' I asked.

'Yes, in the brain, affecting enjoyment, sense of time and performance. Neuroscience has observed certain changes in brains in flow.'

'How does flow work?'

'There are many theories but no incontrovertible explanation,' said Alice. 'It's often that way in psychology, like the Bannister Effect overcame choking. Once Bannister had smashed through the glass ceiling, many other runners performed sub four minute miles.'

'Does it matter how flow works?'

'Could flow be a placebo? If the runner is enjoying her performance and assumes she is in flow, could she go on to a better performance?'

'It can't be ruled out.'

'Flow benefits many facets of performance,' I said.

'He is right,' said Coach Derek. 'I'm sure the flow effect is real. A runner in flow can be so engaged in a race that they forget the pain of running, lose track of time and are surprised how far they've come.'

'I want that,' said Maxi. 'I want to get into flow early and stay there as long as possible.'

'The literature of 'flow' has several types of flow,' said Alice. 'Maxi, you've already experienced the Siri Lindley type, running at the edge, unleashing yourself and smashing through barriers. For 15 kilometres in Brisbane, you ran with total goal commitment. What training do you want to extend it to?'

'During the whole 42 kilometres?'

'It's possible. Siri Lindley used to choke until coach Frank Sutton set her difficult challenges.'

'If Maxi can unleash herself from her past like Siri did, her performance could lift.'

'Siri was angry with her coach for his challenges.'

'Maxi got pretty mad running up that dune before she bonked,' I said. 'Maybe she's already unleashed,'

'Ask me,' said Maxi.

'Are you unleashed Maxi?'

'Yes,' she snarled.

Everyone laughed.

CHAPTER 62 TIME DILATION

'This section is from Chapter 58 in my book *Time is Gold*,' I said. 'It reveals the theory of Special Relativity theory, published by Albert Einstein in 1905. I have explained his theory of the Twins Paradox, a celebrated thought experiment. No-one has ever refuted it. I have written a story which tells how Maxi, the marathoner who runs in flow, wants to improve her performance by time dilation.'

'The Twins Paradox is a thought experiment. Identical twins aged 20 are both marathon runners. One becomes an astronaut and travels in space until she returns to Earth 60 years later. Her speed was very fast, 0.75 of the speed of light. Her 80 years old sister comes to meet her. Only 20 years have passed, as recorded by the spaceship's clock. Events aboard having dilated from 60 to 20 years. At faster speeds, her time would have dilated even more.'

'How could a spaceship travel at 0.75 of the speed of light?' said Dimity. She was an accountant I met at a meeting of our writing group.

'Good question. The fastest we can go is our latest fastest space vehicle, which will go only 430,000 miles per hour. This is only one millionth of the speed of light. The thought experiment is to imagine travel' near the speed of light. Space travel is getting faster and one day we'll reach light speed.'

'Imagine 20 years have passed. When she climbs down from the hatch, she is 20 plus 20 equals 40 years old, comparing with her sister's 80 years. Her physical and mental appearance is consistent with being that much younger. Supposing the traveller has no muscle wastage, the sisters, 80 and 40, could live on Earth and run marathons, adding years to their lives equally by the calendar. The returned traveller could expect to live 40 years longer than her sister, if there was no other effect of her travel.'

'How could one twin sister be physically younger than the other?' asked Dimity.

'The space traveller celebrated 20 birthdays on the correct days, using the ship's clock and calendar, but she has had fewer of them, because the clock was running slower to prevent light speed being exceeded,' I said. 'When she neared the speed of light, her physiology, mind and her whole being would have had more time. Back on Earth again, her decline would resume at the same rate as other 40 year olds.'

'On the spaceship, did her life slow, delay, truncate, decompress, expand, or what?' asked someone.

'None of the those,' I said. 'Her body processes worked the same as usual with the clock running slower.'

'Would she be in slow motion by the on-board clock?'

'No,' I said. 'She would be moving around the same as on Earth without being aware that her clock was running slower.'

'What about if they saw her from Earth through a porthole?'

'She would be in slow motion, one third normal speed. Astronauts on the International Space Station are ageing just a bit slower than people on Earth', I said. 'The astronaut who runs around a track inside the spaceship would finish a 42 kilometres race in first place.'

'The traveller can complete a greater distance inside in dilated time, as with the dogleg path of a light pulse reflected by a mirror inside the spaceship. whose arrival coincides. Observed through a porthole, she's running in slow motion with longer seconds, going further and faster.'

'But Maxi does not have a spaceship!' said Dimity.

'Her impulses are inside something travelling very fast. Maxi's nervous system is like a spaceship. Signals travel very fast from her brain to her legs and back again through tissue pathways. Her neural system is like a spaceship. The signal speeds are fast and cause her time to dilate relative to her reflex time. We can't see inside brains or neurones and measure signal speeds, so it is not scientific, but it is logical and plausible by Einstein's philosophy. The credibility of the thought experiment rests on analogy and intuition. Psychologists often speculate by analogy and modern physics does too. We'll see later that there is evidence that time dilation occurs in the brain. It's a real effect and Maxi can use it to get an edge on rivals.'

'Would her brain impulses travel at the speed of light?'

'The maximum speed through neurones and synapses would be slower, about 430 kilometres per hour, fast enough for time to dilate. When she is stoked, with her brain nearing overload, the speed in her nervous pathway could near this maximum and her response times could dilate, as they would inside the spaceship near light speed. An observer would see her taking less time, using less energy and finishing earlier, like the astronaut.'

'Whoa. My brain is overloaded,' said Dimity. 'Suppose the twin runners are equally talented and the traveller running in the spaceship arrives back at the mid-point of an endurance race in less time. If we suppose the two sisters continue with the second part of their runs, the traveller will finish earlier than her sister, because she will have saved 40 years in the first half, would be younger and would have conserved more energy.'

'Correct,' I said. 'You have brought the thought experiment back to Earth, with a prediction that could be tested. How could her brain be caused to overload?'

'Could she max out?' asked Blake. 'Maxi by name and maxi by nature. When there is heaps of action, her brain can only take in so much before it reaches overload.'

'Nerve impulses travel very fast and have a maximum speed, like light,' Jason said. He was a physics teacher. 'The neural system has a limit. I have heard that stimulus overload can cause a brain to shut down.'

'Before shut down can be reached, her nervous system would become congested and reach peak capacity,' said Alice. 'Mihaly described 'flow' as a condition of full cognitive engagement. It could be the same thing as time dilation.'

'Mihaly's full engagement sounds like a fade-out, whereas Jason's overload is like blowing a fuse,' I said. 'Which would Maxi experience?'

'A runner with brain overload could go either way, into a frazzle or into flow,' Jason said. 'One way is dysfunctional and the other is bliss.'

'Why bliss?' asked Maxi.

'By eliminating stress.'

'How could she do that?'

'By going into flow,' said Alice. 'Her time could dilate, allowing her to complete actions without fading out or jamming.'

'There you have it,' I said. 'That's the last part of my theory.'

'It makes sense,' said Derek, an evolutionary biologist. 'It is an alternative to pumping adrenalin for a fight or flight response.'

'I suppose that's how flow could have evolved,' I said.

'It explains the timelessness everyone talks about with flow,' said Maxi. 'Is there a simpler explanation?'

'Yes,' said Stan. 'When running is enjoyable, time flies and runners rationalize they are 'in flow'.'

'That doesn't explain how they perform better in flow,' I said.

'Are you sure they do?' Stan asked.

'Do you perform better in flow Maxi?' I asked.

'Yes. In London, I was in flow during most of the race. It was my PB.'

'Other explanations are possible, such as training hard.'

'If you continue to win running in flow, we will be convinced.'

'More convinced, yes.'

'It's an interesting story,' said Jason.

'I don't get it,' said Dimity. 'Just because Einstein describes time dilation in space doesn't mean that it will occur in a person's nervous system. It's far-fetched.'

'It's science fiction,' I said. 'Science fiction hasn't happened yet, but it could happen.'

'It is unlikely,' said Dimity.

I resented Dimity's criticism of my analogy, because I had no evidence to contradict her. My argument had a hole in it.

That was the end of discussion and it was serious loss of face for me as a science fiction writer. After that, I felt awkward with Dimity and we stopped going out. I found another writing group.

CHAPTER 63 GOVERNING CLIMATES

The campaign to keep emissions of carbon gases to net zero in 2050 hasn't been tried before. In this final chapter I will collect philosophies and viewpoints referred to earlier which amplify the uncertainty of the venture.

I am a climate science sceptic and engineer. I am not convinced that carbon gases cause climate change. Nor am I a denier: when there is evidence I believe it.

The Australian government has adopted climate policies purportedly to benefit foreign nations on the other side of the world, without requiring a definite benefit here. There would be only circumstantial evidence. Changes in climate have been attributed to carbon emissions by supposition. Warming of climates also by anthropomorphic heat emissions could reasonably be claimed. The amounts of warming by bushfires and geothermal processes has been significant. Melting of glacier ice can also be attributed to variations in precipitation of snow in polar catchments.

Despite water finding a common level, there has been no universal sea level increase because the constant ebb and flow of tides prevents accurate measurement. Universal increase would contradict local effects predicted by plate tectonics.

Global warming is not universal. Temperature effects are not uniform trends, are subject to analytical exaggeration and are removed at night by radiation of heat into space. Energy released by domestic and industrial energy users is small but significant. Control of climate temperature by limiting heat emissions and carbon gas emissions would be more effective than by proscribing carbon emissions.

Analysis of climates for governments' action cannot model climate systems, because Earth's subsurface processes, ocean circulation and chemistry, and circulation of the atmosphere with the seasons, are too extensive to be simplified. Partial models can be developed piecemeal, but conclusions would be highly qualified and probabilistic.

Nevertheless climate science has modelled climate changes determinedly.

'This is the era of central planning. . . The ministers change, but the logic remains. In Australia, the answer is always another central government plan.'
Spectator, August 2025.

In the absence of accurate and trusted modelling, governing of climates could be conducted with anecdotal narratives. In the past, these have aimed for emotional appeal in media.

When models are simulacra, Baudrillard's admonition stands:

'The media represents a world that is more real than reality that we can experience. People lose the ability to distinguish between reality and fantasy.'

For some Australians, the government fantasy presented in the media is a source of satisfaction, when it is an acutely tentative embarrassment, a spectacle foisted on the audience to obtain revenue from advertising products and political votes, as Debord's philosophy explains.

Debord writes that The Society of the Spectacle is an inverted image of society in which relations between commodities have supplanted relations between people.

'Passive identification with the spectacle supplants genuine activity. The spectacle is not a collection of images, rather it is a social relation among people, mediated by images.'

Baudrillard argued we do not live in a 'Global Village', to use Marshall McLuhan's phrase, but rather in a world that is ever more easily petrified by even the smallest event.

Because the 'global' world operates at the level of the exchange of signs and commodities, it becomes ever more blind to symbolic acts, such as, for example, terrorism.

Girard explained a group can be persecuted as the source of disorder and be venerated as the source of order as a god, by the scapegoat mechanism. Fossil fuel use could be blamed for climate change.

These social effects explain the government of climate change and societal adaptation. There was always adventuring to capture people's interest and security in precautions advised by leaders.

CHAPTER 64 CLOSING THE SHORT

When I first arrived at university, I soon had a girlfriend, Bridget, but I was uncomfortable settling down with her. I seemed locked into a paradigm for a man ten years older. Then I met Vicki and set my heart on her. Because she was elusive, I had a comic ploy to sell her to my friend Richard, by commodifying her. But it didn't work. I allowed him to intervene between me and Vicki. He had wanted her because I did and I had wanted her because he did. Girard had described this outcome as mimetic desire, with Richard as mediator. He had falsely promoted finality of my relationship with her.

On the rebound I became entangled with Barbara as a sex partner and I escaped to Canada. I heard from Vicki intermittently over many years. I pursued outcomes in the UK, then emigrated to Australia and adventured in foreign parts.

Vicki had let me down on a couple of occasions when it was evident that I was not in the forefront of her affections, which could have resulted from me chasing other girls. I seemed to not conform to her expectation of monogamy.

When I wrote a novel about commodifying her, it was a satire and contained satirical references to her. She found it intrusive. My book declared my characters were fictional and of course I used different names and descriptions. A couple of scenes had Vicki doing sex with mediators. I was not overly concerned, because I first heard Vicki complain 57 years after the supposed event.

I stayed in touch with Vicki but she wasn't amenable and I took up with Rita, who I married. We had two children and lived in Australia.

Vicki never married until much later and I used to visit her when I returned to the UK. We got on well and I wanted to be with her, but the pull of fathering my two children was greater. I put my family first. Eventually, when my daughters left home, Rita and I separated. When I went to Vicki, I found she had recently married without warning.

I had a string of women friends, but my old romance with Vicki had my attention.

Imagine my surprise when Vicki wrote to me that she was coming to Australia to see me, with her new husband. I realised then that I had told myself the biggest lie: that she didn't want me. But I didn't know how our friendship lay with her husband now.

Her visit was delayed by Covid 19 and as I waited I felt conflict building between us. A difficulty was that I had written a memoir satirising our love, presenting it as a commodity and exaggerating our intimacy from wishful thinking. I wondered if she would demand I withdraw publication of the book. I wondered what her husband's reaction to my fantasy would be. He was an engineer like me. I had behaved honourably enough but he might champion her complaint. It seemed like an ugly scene to me and I wrote back that I didn't want to see her. I couldn't bear conflict and I wanted to avoid any aftermath of her fling with Richard. He was still present, invisibly. I didn't want him to mediate anymore. Our friendship was ended. He had purchased my short and had let it expire, without taking delivery from me.

It was a sad ending to our long adventure. Vicki came to Australia and left without meeting me. I felt used, although I had no reason to believe she had misled me. She could have levelled with me, although she had loyalties that would make it difficult.

I had inferred that Vicki and I had suspended our desire. If I had been a risk taker, I would have pursued it. Because Vicki was a psychologist, I didn't know what I would be getting into. I had spent too long waiting and her price was still too high.

This was a tale of unrequited love. I had imagined that yearning could bring us together and she was concerned not to wreck my marriage and family life. My preoccupation was always my job and I was usually in the wrong place to have a relationship with her.

I always had the feeling that Vicki was not sure of me and that could be interpreted from my pursuit of other women and possibly a suspicion as a psychologist that I would be affected by mental illness, when I was a PhD student.

Vicki came with her husband to Australia after a long interval, expressly about the book I had written. She opposed my basing a character on her. I declined to meet or talk with her. Our first involvement had been for her to have me strapped into a lie detector and now 60 years later, my distrust lingered.

END

BIBLIOGRAPHY

Martin Knox, *Brisbane River Anti-Memoir*, 2023
Martin Knox, *Nanny State*, 2024
Martin Knox, *$hort of Love*, 2019
Neil Strauss, *The Game,* Text, 2005
Mihaly Csikszentmihalyi, *Flow*, 1990
Martin Knox, *Time is Gold*, 2020

www.ingramcontent.com/pod-product-compliance
Lightning Source LLC
Chambersburg PA
CBHW072013070526
44583CB00015B/1459